PLAIN ANSWERS

about the

AMISH LIFE

MINDY STARNS
CLARK

HARVEST HOUSE PUBLISHERS
EUGENE, OREGON

Unless otherwise indicated, all Scriptures are taken from the Holy Bible, New International Version®, NIV®. Copyright © 1973, 1978, 1984, 2011, by Biblica, Inc.™ Used by permission of Zondervan. All rights reserved worldwide. www.zondervan.com

Verses marked KJV are taken from the King James Version of the Bible.

Cover by Dugan Design Group, Bloomington, Minnesota

Cover photos © Tamara Kulikova / Fotolia; iStockphoto / PatriciaPix, JoeLena

Illustrations by Amy Hanson Starns

Mindy Starns Clark is represented by MacGregor Literary, Inc. of Hillsboro, Oregon.

PLAIN ANSWERS ABOUT THE AMISH LIFE
Some of this material appeared in *A Pocket Guide to Amish Life*
Copyright © 2010/2013 by Mindy Starns Clark
Published by Harvest House Publishers
Eugene, Oregon 97408
www.harvesthousepublishers.com

Library of Congress Cataloging-in-Publication Data
    Clark, Mindy Starns.
    [Pocket guide to Amish life]
    Plain answers about the Amish life / Mindy Starns Clark.
        pages cm.
    ISBN 978-0-7369-5593-5 (pbk.)
    ISBN 978-0-7369-5594-2 (eBook)
    Includes bibliographical references and index.
    Part One. Foundation — Defining the Amish — Beliefs — Community — Separation — Nonresistance — Organization — Leadership — Worship — Rules — Shunning — History — Expansion — Part Two. Lifestyle — Amish Life — Food — Health — Clothing and Grooming — Language — Technology — Transportation — Occupations — Free Time, Vacations, and Entertainment — Part Three. Passages — Childhood, Family, and Old Age — School — Rumspringa — Baptism — Courtship and Marriage — Death — Part Four. Outside World — Us and Them — Tourism and the Media — Tragedy and Forgiveness — Why Are They Amish? — What Can They Teach Us? — Part Five. Supplemental Material — Myths Versus Facts — Biblical References.
    Includes bibliographical references and index.
    1. Amish—United States—Social life and customs. 2. Peace—Religious aspects—Amish. 3. Amish—Doctrines. I. Title.
    E184.M45C53 2013
    289.7'73—dc23
                                                                                    2013000683

Printed in the United States of America

21 22 23 24 25 / VP-JH / 10 9 8 7 6 5 4 3

*This book is dedicated to the Amish,
with thanks for all they have taught me about the need for
surrender, submission, separation, and simplicity
in my own Christian walk.*

ACKNOWLEDGMENTS

My husband, John, for always, for everything.

Our two daughters, Emily and Lauren, who never cease to amaze me with their kindness, generosity, and resourcefulness.

My gifted editor and friend, Kim Moore, and all of the lovely folks at Harvest House Publishers, especially LaRae Weikert, Barb Sherrill, and Bob Hawkins Jr., who encouraged me to explore Amish life in new ways.

Amy Starns, whose beautiful artwork graces the pages of this book.

Stephanie Ciner, Dee Benjamin, Chip MacGregor, ChiLibris, and all the members of my online advisory group, Consensus.

Everyone who helped facilitate my research into Amish life, including Erik Wesner, Dave Siegrist, and the Mennonite Information Center in Lancaster, Pennsylvania.

A portion of the proceeds from this book will be donated to Amish-related nonprofit organizations. Visit www.amishfaqs.com/behind.php for more information.

CONTENTS

Foreword 7

How to Use This Book 11

PART ONE: FOUNDATION

1. Defining the Amish 15
2. Beliefs 19
3. Community 25
4. Separation 29
5. Nonresistance 33
6. Organization 35
7. Leadership 37
8. Worship 41
9. Rules 45
10. Shunning 49
11. History 53
12. Expansion 57

PART TWO: LIFESTYLE

13. Amish Life 63
14. Food 69
15. Health 73
16. Clothing and Grooming 77
17. Language 83
18. Technology 87
19. Transportation 93
20. Occupations 97
21. Free Time, Vacations, and Entertainment 99

Part Three: Passages

22. Childhood, Family, and Old Age 105

23. School 109

24. *Rumspringa* 113

25. Baptism 117

26. Courtship and Marriage 121

27. Death 125

Part Four: Outside World

28. Us and Them 129

29. Tourism and the Media 131

30. Tragedy and Forgiveness 137

31. Why Are They Amish? 141

32. What Can The Amish Teach Us? 145

Part Five: Supplemental Material

Biblical References for Amish Beliefs
and Practices 151

Bibliography 153

Resources 157

Index 159

Notes 173

FOREWORD

Why are we so fascinated with the Amish? If we're not marveling at their enchanting dress and simple lifestyle, we're grappling with their unusual practices and austere ways. Our curiosity mingles with admiration, confusion, and suspicion. Just who are these people? Why do they live this way?

And why do we care so much?

Without a doubt, the Amish ignite our curiosity. We buy Amish-made products, cook Amish recipes, and read Amish fiction. We take vacations to what we call "Amish country," those Amish-heavy regions such as Lancaster County, Pennsylvania, and Holmes County, Ohio. While there, we look for glimpses of them from our cars and discreetly snap photographs from a distance. We wonder what it would be like to live without constant interruptions, the stresses of modern life, and the intrusions of technology. Once in a while, we think we might like to be one of them, to live as they do.

Usually, those thoughts pass just as quickly as they come, for we know we couldn't survive without television, without e-mail, without driving. We don't really want to be one of them, and yet the allure remains. The Amish themselves don't always understand our attraction either, but in response a wise Amish man once issued the following challenge:

> *If you admire our faith, strengthen yours.*
> *If you admire our sense of commitment, deepen yours.*
> *If you admire our community spirit, build one.*
> *If you admire the simple life, cut back.*
> *If you admire quality merchandise or land stewardship,*
>   *then make quality.*
> *If you admire deep character and enduring values, live them.*

This popular saying is frequently posted on the walls of restaurants and tourist attractions in Amish country. The first time I saw it, I understood why its message was so important. We can't all be Amish, but in many ways, we would do well to follow their example.

Unfortunately, that's not always easy to do. Given the vast proliferation of Amish-related myths, inaccuracies, and outright fallacies that are out there—online, in print, in the movies, and more—it's easy to misunderstand even the most basic facts about the Amish. The goal of this book is to clear up many of those misconceptions by providing accurate information about these people and the lives they lead.

In these pages I have chosen to focus primarily on the largest and most well-known affiliation, the Old Order Amish. Practices vary, however, so in order to avoid definitive statements that do not hold true for all Amish affiliations, or even for all Old Order districts, I use words such as "usually" and "most" and "many" whenever describing Amish life and regulations.

Finally, though the Amish have terms to describe those who are not Amish—such as "English" or "fancy"—I will most often use "non-Amish" and "outsider." These seem appropriate because this guide is looking in on Amish life from the outside rather than the other way around.

Living near Lancaster County myself, I have developed great respect for the Amish over the years. Though I could never live as they do, I understand why it works for them. I do not see them through rose-colored glasses, nor do I pass judgment on their more incomprehensible regulations. The subject is so complex, in fact, that for this book I have chosen simply to observe, question, read, study, watch, interview, and report. This process has confirmed to me that while the Amish themselves are "just people" like the rest of us, their way of life is utterly foreign to our own, the choices they make are unique, and their ways are genuinely worthy of study.

As you read and use this book, I hope you will gain a deeper understanding of the Amish faith, life, and values, and that this will help you to form your own opinions about why you find them so intriguing. Most of all, my prayer is that you will use this new knowledge to enhance your own faith. Thus, may we all be "iron sharpening iron"—Amish, author, and reader—helping one another to grow through a new perspective.

Enjoy!

HOW TO USE THIS BOOK

Plain Answers About the Amish Life is written in a question-and-answer format and is organized by topic into five main sections:

- *Foundation* explains the basis of the Amish faith, including theology, history, organization, church practices and leadership, and demographics.
- *Lifestyle* covers various elements of Amish life that are so different from our own, such as clothing, language, transportation, and the use of technology.
- *Passages* deals with the various stages of growth and transition in life—such as childhood, baptism, marriage, and death—from an Amish perspective.
- *Outside World* presents information about interactions of the Amish with external entities such as media and tourism.
- *Supplemental Material* provides additional resources for further study, including biblical references, contact information for various Amish-related organizations, and a full index.

Much of the information in this book has been gleaned from a previous work of mine, *A Pocket Guide to Amish Life*, which was published in 2010. Using that guide as my starting point, I shaped the text from that book into this all-new Q & A format, expanding and enhancing the material to provide answers to every possible question you might have about the Amish.

Not only is this information even easier to access and understand, but it can be read in any order and referred to again and again. Simply start with the Contents or the Index to find your topic of interest and move around from there. (Note: To enhance this skip-around approach, I have had to include some minor repetition of information where various subjects tend to overlap.) While you can use this book in any order you please, each section does build upon the previous material, so reading it in order may give you an even greater understanding of the Amish and their various beliefs and practices.

Finally, be sure to check out AmishReader on Facebook, which lets you join in the conversation, pose questions of your own, and discover an even wider array of resources about the Amish.

Part One:
FOUNDATION

When I arrived, Christy was sitting under the oak tree, her skirt and apron perfectly arranged, a thick book open on her lap. Nearly every Amish home had a copy of the familiar, massive tome, an account of our ancestors who perished for their faith.

I kneeled beside her. "What do you think of the Martyrs Mirror*?"*

"Bo-ring. History is stupid."

It was quite an unusual statement for a person of our faith to make. From the day we were born, our history was practically born with us. It was a huge part of who we were as a people. I couldn't imagine, for example, that she found boring the story of Dirk Willems, the man who rescued his pursuer who had fallen through ice, only to then be arrested. I said as much, but she merely yawned in response.

"You'll see," I said to her, "history won't be boring on this trip. Not the way I'm going to teach it. It will all be very much alive."

—Excerpted from *The Amish Nanny*
by Mindy Starns Clark and Leslie Gould

1

DEFINING THE AMISH

Who are the Amish?

The Amish are a Christian sect that separated from the Mennonites in seventeenth-century Europe and began emigrating to America in search of religious freedom in the eighteenth century. Now living exclusively in the United States and Canada, the Amish are known, among other things, for their plain dress and plain living, rejection of modern conveniences, and chiefly agrarian society.

Are all Amish groups the same?

No. Due to several centuries of church growth, expansion, and division, many different types of Amish affiliations are now in North America, each with different sets of rules and practices. There are, however, certain elements that most Amish groups tend to have in common, including that they:

- adhere to a statement of faith known as the Eighteen Articles
- wear some form of distinctive Plain clothing
- worship in homes rather than in church buildings
- do not connect their houses with public utilities as a way of remaining separate from the world
- use horses and buggies as their primary means of transportation
- limit formal education to the eighth grade
- live in rural areas
- emphasize an agrarian lifestyle

- are pacifists
- choose their religious leaders through divine appointment by drawing lots
- speak a German dialect as their primary language
- value the history of their people and their martyrs' heritage

In what ways are the various groups different?

While all Amish affiliations adhere to the same basic belief system, the particular ways in which they choose to live out those beliefs can vary greatly from group to group. Aspects on which they may differ include such elements as buggy styles, church discipline, clothing, lawn mowers, technology, and much more.

How many Amish people are there?

Statistics differ among researchers, but according to the Young Center for Anabaptist and Pietist Studies at Elizabethtown College, if we count all family members—including baptized adults and not-yet-baptized infants, children, and teens—the total number comes to almost 300,000 Amish currently living in the United States and Canada.

How are they divided into the different groups?

Though it's difficult to provide an exact number, at least two dozen different Amish affiliations are in North America. (See chapter 6, "Organization," for more information about how the Amish church is structured.) These affiliations are further divided into more than 2000 church districts. Approximately 500 Amish settlements are located in 30 states and in Canada.

Where did the word "Amish" come from?

The word "Amish" first came from the name of Jakob Ammann, an Anabaptist leader who proposed a number of changes to the Mennonite faith in the late 1600s, eventually causing a break in the church. Those who joined him and followed his teachings became known as the "Amish." (See chapter 11, "History," to learn about Ammann and his followers.)

Is that what the word "Amish" means? Someone who is a follower of Jakob Ammann?

That was its original meaning, though it has evolved over the years to indicate that and much more. In fact, the word "Amish" is listed in the dictionary as both a noun (the Amish) and an adjective (Amish farm, Amish furniture, Amish fiction, and so on). Currently, "Amish" indicates a faith culture, a way of life, a set of values, a style of clothing, a collection of technological adaptations, and much more.

The Amish and Mennonites have remained separate groups to this day, though their technology is similar in many ways.

2

BELIEFS

Are the Amish a cult?

No. The Amish are Christians and do not fit the modern, generally accepted criteria for what constitutes a cult. They may be confused as one because they follow a very restrictive set of rules and face excommunication (shunning) for certain infractions of those rules. However, unlike a cult, the Amish faith is not centered on a single human authority, they do not require their members to pool their finances, and the tenets of their faith are compatible with most major Protestant denominations. Thus, they are not a cult but simply an ultraconservative Christian faith culture.

What do the Amish believe, religiously speaking?

The Amish are Christians and adhere to the following tenets of the Christian faith:

> *There is one God.*
> *God is a trinity.*
> *Jesus came to earth as God in the flesh,*
>   *died, and rose again.*
> *Salvation comes through grace by faith.*
> *Scripture is the divinely inspired word of God.*
> *The church is the body of Christ.*

Note that these same beliefs are also held by the Catholic church and by most Protestant denominations as well. The difference between the Amish and other Christian groups is not so much what they believe as it is how they have chosen to live out those beliefs.

If their beliefs aren't all that different from other Christian denominations, then why do the Amish have so many odd practices, such as dressing the way they do and not using electricity?

Most of the elements of the Amish lifestyle that seem unique or confusing are not due to a complicated or controversial theology, but instead to the ways they have chosen to live out their Christian walk in their day-to-day lives. They attempt to follow the teachings of Jesus, particularly the Sermon on the Mount, by emphasizing certain biblical values, including:

- *surrender* of the self-will to God
- *submission* to authority, to the faith community, and to its rules
- *separation* from the world, becoming a "peculiar people" by turning to family and the faith community, by honoring history and tradition, and by turning the other cheek
- *simplicity* through the practice of humility, modesty, thrift, and peacefulness

Jesus embodied these values of surrender, submission, separation, and simplicity throughout His life and thus provided the perfect example of how we, too, should live. A biblical passage frequently cited by the Amish comes from the night before Jesus was crucified, when He exemplified surrender and submission as He knelt in the Garden of Gethsemane and prayed, "Remove this cup from me: nevertheless not my will, but thine, be done" (Luke 22:42 KJV). The Amish

— IN THEIR OWN WORDS —

For the Amish, culture and religion are intertwined to the point where it is hard to separate the two. Indeed, it is a faith culture.

strive to be as obedient in every area of life as Jesus was in that moment. Their many unique lifestyle regulations are based on this overriding goal of Christlikeness.

Is the reason they deny themselves modern comforts to earn their way into heaven?

No. The reason for their lifestyle is not to earn grace. Instead, it comes from a desire to live out a Christlike lifestyle of surrender, submission, separation, and simplicity.

Are you positive they are not trying to "earn" their salvation? Because I've heard conflicting answers to this question. Some Amish say that if they violate the ordinances, they won't get into heaven. That sounds like a works-based religion to me.

As with many denominations, there are factions that teach variations of the core beliefs. While you are correct that some Amish are taught that they must earn their way into heaven, the official Amish belief—and the one held by the majority of Amish groups—is that salvation comes through grace alone.

Do the Amish believe in the concept of salvation? Do they consider themselves "saved" or "born again"?

Yes, the Amish believe in salvation, and many would describe themselves as saved, born again, or as having a personal relationship with Jesus Christ.

Various Amish affiliations seem to be of different minds, however, on the topic of what is known as "assurance of salvation." The majority of Amish believe it would be prideful to state outright that they have received salvation and instead maintain what they call a "living hope" or a "continued effort" on the topic. They trust the ultimate fate of their soul to God's providence rather than claim it with certainty.

There are other Amish groups, however, that feel an assurance of salvation is not prideful but biblical, citing verses such as 1 John 5:13, which says, "I write these things to you who believe in the name of the Son of God so that you may *know* that you have eternal life" (emphasis added). Amish who fall on this side of the topic believe that everyone who has accepted Jesus Christ as their personal Lord and Savior can know with certainty that they have been saved for eternity.

Is there a person or organization that oversees the Amish church the way the pope does for Catholics or the Southern Baptist Convention does for Southern Baptists?

No. Unlike many religious denominations, the Amish have no central authority—no pope, synod, convention, diocese, association, or the like. Instead, the ultimate authority for Amish life and practice lies within each local district. This is why rules can vary from district to district even within an affiliation—each congregation follows the rules established by its own leaders.

The bishops in an affiliation meet together regularly to discuss issues and look for common stances. This provides unity within the affiliation and support for the bishops as they administer their districts.

Do the Amish think theirs is the only one true religion?

No. To do so would be prideful, which goes against one of their most basic values. The Amish are respectful of other Christian denominations. As one Amish man said, the Bible is meant to be a mirror, not a spotlight. Better to pay attention to their own walk with God than presume to judge others'.[1]

If I asked an Amish person how to get to heaven, what would his answer be?

That person would likely refer to God's will in the matter and then perhaps describe the need to have a personal relationship with Christ. He might also quote an applicable Scripture, such as, "Believe in the Lord Jesus, and you will be saved" (Acts 16:31).

Would an Amish person try to convert me to the Amish faith?

No. More than anyone, the Amish know how rare and unusual such a conversion would be for a person who was not raised Amish. He might, however, encourage you to seek out a good church, one more in keeping with your own upbringing or community.

--- IN THEIR OWN WORDS ---

The nice thing is that anyone can choose to be a follower of Christ regardless of his lot in life and the cultural context he lives in. No need to be Amish in order to believe in the Lord and have eternal life—unless, of course, the Lord wants you to be Amish.

May I convert to the Amish faith if I want to?

The Amish allow converts to their faith, though successful, permanent conversions of outsiders into the Amish church are extremely rare. See chapter 28, "Us and Them," for more information.

Do the Amish ever send out missionaries or engage in other mission work?

According to authors Charles Hurst and David McConnell in *An Amish Paradox: Diversity and Change in the World's Largest Amish Community*, "Specific responses to the great commission vary considerably by affiliation, by district, and by individual inclination."[2] For the Amish who do support missions, they are more likely to focus on charity and relief work rather than on witnessing or evangelizing.

Any travel for missions is most often to help out in areas that have been affected by natural disasters and are in need of extensive rebuilding. I once had an interesting conversation with two young Amish men in their early twenties who had gone, hammers in hand, on a mission trip to the Gulf Coast in the wake of Hurricane Katrina.

In some areas, Old Order Amish will donate to or volunteer at Plain-run nonprofit organizations such as the Mennonite Central Committee or Christian Aid Ministries. Hurst and McConnell describe one such organization based in Holmes County, Ohio, where local Amish church districts "send volunteers for 'work days' to can massive amounts of turkey for shipment to Burundi, North Korea, and other sites."[3]

Despite these mission-related activities, most Old Order Amish consider their primary "missions" task to be setting an example in their own lives at home.

COMMUNITY

Why is community so important to the Amish?

Community is the cornerstone of Amish life. This is based on biblical precedent such as that in Acts 2:44: "All the believers were together and had everything in common."

Community is where the Amish most often find their identity, support, lifestyle, worship, classmates, spouses, and friends. It is a source of strength, an insurance policy when disaster strikes, and a safe haven in an often hostile (or at least intrusively curious) world. To the outsider, the extent to which members of the Amish community care for one another is often incomprehensible. To the Amish, it's simply one of the primary values that define their lives.

What do they do to keep their communities so close-knit?

To understand what makes Amish communities so strong, it helps to be aware of the following Amish beliefs:

- The virtue of humility is shown through respect for God and others.
- All persons are worthy of dignity and respect.
- Everyone in the community is accountable to God.
- Communities are made stronger when individuals do not use personal desire as their supreme criteria for making decisions.
- Traditions are more important than progress.
- Accumulated wisdom is better than an individual's ideas.
- Mutual aid benefits everyone and makes the community stronger.

- Authority in all of its various forms is to be obeyed. For example, ministers submit to bishops, members to leaders, wives to husbands, children to parents, students to teachers, and younger to elder.

These beliefs work together to create a strong bond between community members.

What is mutual aid and why is it important?

Mutual aid is when the community provides care, both physically and financially, for members in need.

For example, the Amish do not purchase commercial insurance coverage, believing instead that when difficulty or disaster strikes, the church community members are to step in and help. This principle serves dual purposes: It helps keep the church separate from the world, and it binds the Amish community together and forces them to depend on one another. Some Amish communities have organized their own official insurance programs, though others handle members' needs on a less formal basis.

What are some other examples of mutual aid?

Some examples of mutual aid would be when:

- members face large hospital bills they cannot afford, and the community pays the bills for them
- a building burns down, and the community erects a new one
- someone dies, and the community steps in to help with the funeral arrangements and take over all farm and household chores for several days
- another community suffers a natural disaster, and other communities come in to help rebuild
- a farmer is injured, and the community takes over his farmwork until he gets better

Is that why they do barn raisings?

Yes. Perhaps the biggest symbol of the Amish community in action is the well-known barn raising. These events involve hundreds of Amish working together for a single day. In about nine hours, they can construct an oak beam-and-peg barn that will last for generations. The Amish use their barns for farmwork, storing feed and grain, sheltering livestock, and housing valuable tools. Barns are also social centers where large gatherings—such as church services, funerals, marriages, and baptisms—may be held if the home is too small.

How does an Amish barn raising work?

Author Erik Wesner describes this interesting process in his blog, AmishAmerica.com, as follows:

> Barn raisings require organization, supplies, and labor. They are typically led by one or two master Amish "engineers" who lay out plans for the barn and assure the materials are available. Supplies and livestock may be donated by fellow church members. All labor is contributed for free as well. Amish know they may be in need of the community's help themselves one day.

> Typically the blocks and cement used in the foundation are laid before the day of the actual raising, allowing time to dry and set. The day of the barn raising, men arrive early. The master organizes men and instructs on jobs, overseeing the whole event. Amish traditionally build barns using wood-peg mortise and tenon joint construction, but may also use more modern materials and techniques.

> Despite the common belief that Amish do the whole job in a single day, it may take a week or more from start to finish. There are typically a good bit of preparations

to be done beforehand as well. However, the wood frame structure usually does go up in one day.

Women help by preparing meals for the men. Youth and children participate as well. Hundreds typically attend, either as workers, support, or observers.[1]

Are there any drawbacks to living in such a tight-knit community?

As with any social group, pluses and minuses exist in Amish community life. On the minus side, such a tight-knit, mutually accountable arrangement can sometimes lead to intrusiveness, quick leaps to judgment, and gossip. On the plus side, one can always find friendship, fellowship, comfort, help, accountability, and more close at hand.

Other than letters from relatives or friends, how do the Amish keep up with what's happening in various communities across the country?

The most common way to keep up with Amish-related news throughout the United States is with the *Budget*, a popular nationwide newspaper headquartered in Ohio that prints and distributes reports of local happenings sent in by a far-flung network of Amish scribes. In this way, the sense of Amish community is encouraged and nurtured despite the distances and differences between the various settlements. To many Amish, reading the *Budget* is like sitting down over coffee with a friend to hear the latest news, even if that news is happening many states away. Visit the *Budget*'s website at www.thebudgetnewspaper.com.

Another popular publication among the Amish is *The New American Almanac*, or as it's often called, *Raber's Almanac*. Updated yearly, this nondescript little book includes a listing of all Amish ministers, their names, addresses, and dates of birth, death, and ordination, all organized by state, county, and church district.[2]

4

SEPARATION

Why do the Amish keep to themselves so much?

One of the core elements of the Amish faith is that Christians are to be *in* the world but not *of* the world. Many Amish practices are based on this principle, both in the ways they separate themselves from their non-Amish surroundings and in the ways they turn toward one another as a faith community.

On what do they base that practice?

On such Bible verses as Romans 12:2, which says, "Do not conform to the pattern of this world, but be transformed by the renewing of your mind." The Amish interpret verses like this to mean that they are to be different from the world in all parts of their lives—not only in thought but also in appearance and actions.

Is it true that one reason they keep to themselves is because they fear persecution?

We will see in chapter 11, "History," that many of the early Anabaptists suffered persecution, torture, and death because of their beliefs, creating the "martyr tradition" on which the Amish faith was founded. Over the years they have suffered through other periods of (less heinous) persecution. For example, their status as pacifist conscientious objectors made them easy targets for bullying, derision, and other kinds of torment in times of war.

Though general sentiments toward the Amish have drastically changed over the years, this history of persecution nevertheless reinforced the Amish belief in a necessary division between the kingdoms of this world, which they say use laws and violence and coercion, and the kingdom of God, which is peaceful, loving, and kind.

What sorts of things do they do to keep themselves "separate" from the world?

The Amish convey their separation from society through specific acts both large and small, such as having:

- no electrical or telephone lines to Amish homes, as that would physically connect them with the outside world
- a unique style of dress, transportation, and other cultural markers that identify them as a unified group while also demonstrating their separation from the world
- limits on certain kinds of technology that may have a negative impact on the Amish home or church
- a directive to settle conflicts between believers within the structure of the church rather than the legal system or the government
- limits on outside monetary dependence, such as commercial insurance coverage

When examining a particular peculiarity of the Amish lifestyle, viewing it in the light of their determination to remain separate from the world often helps make sense of confusing, seemingly arbitrary rules and regulations.

Do the Amish pay taxes?

The Amish pay all taxes that the non-Amish do, including income tax, property tax, sales tax, and estate tax. Though they support the public school system with their taxes, in most cases they are also paying fees to fund their own private Amish schools as well.

The only taxes from which they can choose to be exempt for religious purposes are Social Security and, in some states, workers' compensation. The Amish view both programs as forms of insurance, in which they generally do not participate. Instead, they prefer to follow the biblical directive to provide financially for one another in times of crisis rather than accept money from the government.

Why do the Amish object to insurance?

The Amish eschew commercial insurance coverage for several reasons, primarily because:

- The Bible says we are to care for one another.
- They feel it creates too strong of a connection with the world.
- Mutual financial dependence strengthens community bonds.

In times of crisis, some Amish communities administer financial aid via their own official, organized insurance programs, while others handle needs on a less formal basis.

Do the Amish vote?

According to Donald Kraybill in *The Riddle of Amish Culture*, voting is not common among the Amish, though neither is it usually prohibited outright. In most congregations, the decision is left to the individual.[1] Of the Amish who do choose to vote, they are more likely to participate in local elections than national ones, and then only if matters will directly affect them, such as zoning issues.

The two main reasons that the Amish generally abstain from voting are:

1. They see it as a form of interacting with the world, but they are to maintain a separation from the world.
2. As believers in nonresistance, they are reluctant to cast votes for any official who would then be in a position to utilize force on the nation's behalf.

Though less than 15 percent of Amish are likely to vote in any presidential election, many follow and discuss political events and form opinions.

Do the Amish belong to unions?

No. Generally, they consider unions to be coercive and thus a violation of Jesus's admonishment to turn the other cheek (Matthew 5:39).

Do the Amish participate in lawsuits?

For the most part, the Amish steer clear of litigation, also in obedience to Jesus's directive in Matthew 5:39 to turn the other cheek. Matters involving situations of material interest, such as business disputes or investment losses, are generally settled within the community or surrendered to "God's will."

In some cases, when it comes to issues that challenge their beliefs, the Amish will agree to litigation. In 1972, for example, they fought for the freedom to establish their own educational limits. The case went all the way to the Supreme Court, where the Amish—and other religious minorities—were given the right to discontinue children's education after the eighth grade.

If an Amish person is sued by a non-Amish person or entity, they will usually defend their interests, though they would prefer to reach a settlement than go to court.

Do the Amish hold political office?

No. To do so would create too strong of a connection with the world, not to mention that it could compromise the Amish stance on passive resistance.

Can an Amish person be friends with someone who isn't Amish?

Absolutely. Though the Amish maintain a general separation from the world, many have friendships with non-Amish. Once trust has been established, strong bonds are often forged with neighbors and other townspeople. Repeated business interactions can also cause solid, long-lasting relationships to form over time.

As one Amish man said, "We treasure friendships of all kinds, provided our respective identities are not challenged and ripped down."

5

NONRESISTANCE

Why don't the Amish serve in the military?

Because of Bible verses such as Exodus 20:13 (KJV), "Thou shalt not kill" and Matthew 5:39, "If anyone slaps you on the right cheek, turn to them the other cheek also," the Amish believe force should never be used in any human relations whatsoever, for any reason. This is why they do not serve in the military nor practice any form of self-defense. It is also why they won't work as police officers, hold political office, or serve on juries.

What do the Amish do when a law conflicts with their religious beliefs?

When a civic law conflicts with Amish beliefs, they follow the example of the apostles, who said, "We must obey God rather than human beings!" (Acts 5:29). Historically, this has put them in some very uncomfortable situations and, in some cases, has even forced them to defend their positions in court. In the United States, the Amish have conflicted with local, state, and federal governments over issues of education, military service, property zoning, child labor, Social Security, health care, photo identification, road safety, and more.

If they have no central religious authority, how do they present a united front to lawmakers?

In 1967, the National Amish Steering Committee was formed to address legal issues involving state and federal governments. By working through this committee and living under the American political system, which protects freedom of religion, the Amish have managed to carve out exceptions, work through negotiations, and establish understandings with the government on many topics. These agreements have allowed them to continue their lifestyle with relatively few compromises.

In practice, that means while people in some settlements may be required to display reflective triangles or tape on the backs of their buggies for safety purposes, they are also able to register as conscientious objectors, exempt themselves from Social Security, teach their children in their own private schools, and allow those children to complete their schooling at the end of the eighth grade.

6

ORGANIZATION

How is Amish society organized?

Amish society can be viewed in terms of units. Beyond the most important unit, which is the family, there are also settlements, districts, and affiliations.

What is an Amish settlement?

A settlement is a cluster of Amish living within a common geographical area. Beliefs and practices can vary widely within a single settlement, particularly in those that are the most densely populated. (A settlement can have less than 100 people or more than 30,000.) Statistics vary among researchers, but the Young Center for Anabaptist and Pietist Studies estimates that there are 463 settlements existing in the United States and Canada. The three largest settlements in the country are in Holmes County, Ohio; Lancaster County, Pennsylvania; and Elkhart/LaGrange, Indiana.

What is an Amish district?

A district is a group of Amish who live near one another and worship together, somewhat like a congregation or a parish. Districts average about 135 people (20 to 40 families), and as membership and families grow, new districts are created by dividing existing districts. Statistics vary, but estimates show that there are approximately 2000 church districts in the United States and Canada.

Why do the Amish divide larger districts into smaller ones?

Districts are kept to a certain size for several reasons, including:

- so that members can continue to meet within homes (the Amish hold services and other functions in houses or barns rather than in church buildings)
- to maintain spiritual intimacy
- to prevent any one district from becoming too powerful or, more importantly, too prideful

How are the districts divided?

District boundaries are usually defined along geographical markers, such as streams and roads. In more densely populated Amish settlements, it is not unheard of for across-the-street neighbors (even if they are close relatives) to belong to different districts.

What is an affiliation?

An affiliation is a collection of districts with similar lifestyle regulations and cooperative relationships among their leaders. Affiliations are not defined by geography but by practices and beliefs. Roughly 25 different Amish affiliations exist in the United States and Canada.

Do members of the different groups associate with one another?

As long as they are in the same affiliation, members of different districts can fellowship, attend one another's church services, intermarry, and even exchange ministers and share bishops. Though rules and practices may vary somewhat from district to district, the districts in an affiliation follow practices and beliefs that are similar enough to allow such interaction.

7

LEADERSHIP

How are Amish church districts structured?

Amish church leadership includes three positions: bishop, minister, and deacon. These leaders serve at the district level, which is where the ultimate authority lies within the Amish faith. They work individually and together to guide the actions of their district.

What does an Amish bishop do?

The bishop is the primary spiritual leader of the district. Most bishops serve one district, except in Lancaster County, which is so densely populated that one bishop usually serves two districts. Some of the bishop's duties include:

- conducting congregational meetings, baptisms, communions, weddings, ordinations, and funerals
- interpreting and enforcing district regulations
- resolving matters of disobedience, discipline, and dispute
- recommending excommunication or reinstatement when necessary
- serving as interim bishop to neighboring districts when needed
- preaching in some Sunday services

What does an Amish minister do?

Most districts have two or three ministers. Though their primary duty is to preach in services, they are also involved in:

- serving as role models for the congregation

- helping to maintain the spiritual welfare of the district
- assisting the bishop in his various duties (listed above)

Though ministers will usually prepare for their Sunday sermons by studying the Bible—in both English and German—and referring to various study aids such as concordances, the sermons themselves are given extemporaneously, without any notes.

— IN THEIR OWN WORDS —

The fact that ministers are chosen from among
the members by the use of the divine lot
eliminates a great deal of politics, a fact that
I personally greatly appreciate.

What does an Amish deacon do?

Most districts have just one deacon, who performs various duties, including:

- reading Scripture or reciting prayer in worship services
- supervising the financial aid of the church
- assisting with baptisms and communion
- investigating rule violations in the congregation
- delivering news of excommunication or reinstatement to parties involved
- serving as the church's representative in the facilitation of marriages

Do women have a voice in the Amish church?

Yes. Though church leaders are always male, the women of the church participate in the voting processes and in the nomination of leaders.

Most experts consider the Amish to be a "patriarchal democracy," which means that while only males serve in positions of authority, women have a voice in certain matters. When a decision needs to be made, the bishop gives a recommendation, and the full congregation—male and female—votes on it.

How are ministers chosen in the Amish church?

The Amish choose potential ministers by nominating candidates from among male members of the congregation. Nominees who receive the required number of votes then draw lots to determine which one of them will take on the position.

How are bishops chosen?

Just as with ministers, bishops are chosen by lot, though nominees come from the pool of eligible ministers rather than from the congregation at large.

Why are Amish leaders chosen by drawing lots?

The Amish base this practice on "divine appointment," as shown in Acts 1:24-26, when the apostles used this method to choose a replacement for Judas.

How does the drawing of lots work?

The choosing of lots is usually done on a communion Sunday. A Bible verse is written on a piece of paper and then hidden inside a hymnbook. That hymnbook is mixed with several others, and each nominee chooses one. The man who chooses the hymnbook that has the verse inside is the new leader.

What is it like to be a leader in the Amish church?

Leaders have no formal theological training, and they serve for life without financial remuneration. They spend a lot of time and effort on their duties, employing diplomacy, dealing with difficult issues, and sometimes making unpopular decisions that impact the entire group. Thus, despite the honor of being nominated, many dedicated, godly Amish men prefer *not* to be chosen as a leader. The amount of time and energy required to fulfill their leadership commitments can have a negative impact on their work and farms. Still, most accept the mantle with grace, following the example of Christ in saying, "Not my will, but thine, be done" (Luke 22:42 KJV).

8

WORSHIP

What is an Amish church service like?

Old Order worship services generally open with a hymn sung slowly, in unison, without instruments. As the congregation sings, the bishop and ministers gather in a different room and decide who will preach the opening sermon and who will preach the main sermon. Besides congregational singing, services feature Scripture reading, silent prayer, and spoken prayer read from a prayer book. The opening sermon comes next, and it is given without the aid of any notes. This is followed by the main sermon, which is also given extemporaneously. When the main sermon is over, other ministers may add input or correction as they feel led.

How long does all of that take?

Amish church services last about three hours. The opening sermon is about 20 to 30 minutes long, and the main sermon can last an hour or more.

What language is used in church?

Hymns, Scripture readings, and spoken prayers are in High German. Sermons are given in Pennsylvania Dutch.

Do they offer children's programs on Sunday mornings?

No. The entire family worships together. From the youngest to the oldest, everyone is expected to sit still and pay attention despite the length of the service, the use of the less-familiar High German in the songs and prayers and readings, the hard wooden benches, and any seasonal discomfort, such as summer heat or winter chill.

During church, congregations usually sit divided by gender and age, though very young children will sit with a parent.

How often do the Amish go to church?

Amish worship services are usually held every other Sunday. On the alternating Sundays they may spend quiet family time at home, gather with others for informal readings from the Bible, or attend the services of a different district in their affiliation. No work is done on Sundays except that which is absolutely necessary, such as the care and feeding of the animals.

Is it true they hold church services in their homes?

Yes. Most Amish do not use church buildings, but instead they rotate services among the homes in a district. If a house is not large enough to accommodate the entire congregation, a service may be held in a barn, basement, or large shop. Each Amish family hosts the service about once a year, depending on the size of the district. For congregational seating, the district provides hard, wooden benches that are delivered to the host home the day before on a special wagon that has been designed for just that purpose.

The church service is often followed by a light communal meal, also in the host home.

Do they observe communion?

Yes. Twice a year, in spring and fall, the Amish will hold a special communion service that includes foot washing. This event is usually preceded by a council meeting and concludes with an offering of alms for the needy. This special day can last up to eight hours and is usually a time of rejoicing and renewal for the entire congregation.

What sort of theological training does the church provide?

Formal religious training is provided prior to baptism through an eight- or nine-week program taught by the bishop and ministers. Beyond that, churches usually don't offer such things as Sunday school, children's programs, or youth retreats. In fact, the Old Order Amish rarely deal with discussions or teachings of formal theology at all—in the church, home, or school. Instead, their emphasis is on the practice of faith in action through surrender, submission, separation, and simplicity in their day-to-day lives. As the Amish saying goes, "Learn obedience first, and the rest will follow."

What hymnals do they use in church?

All music sung in the Amish church comes from the *Ausbund*, a songbook containing hymns written by early Anabaptists. The *Ausbund* contains lyrics only; the tunes are passed down from one generation to the next. These lyrics are written in High German.

All hymns are sung a cappella as no instruments are played during church services.

Do they prefer one particular version of the Bible?

In church services, they use the German Martin Luther Bible. Outside of church, they are more likely to read from the King James Version, though some may use the New International Version as well.

9

RULES

Why do the Amish have so many rules?

The Amish believe that setting limits and respecting them are keys to Christlikeness, wisdom, and fulfillment. To them, regulations shape identity, build community, help prevent temptation, and provide a sense of belonging. Without rules, which are defined in what's known as the *Ordnung*, they feel that one can fall prey to pride, unhappiness, insecurity, loss of dignity, and ultimately self-destruction.

What is the *Ordnung*?

The *Ordnung* is what the Amish call the set of rules and regulations that dictate their day-to-day lives. The *Ordnung* deals with a wide variety of topics, such as clothing, transportation, technology, education, and much more.

To join the Amish church, one must agree to abide by all the rules of the *Ordnung*.

Is the *Ordnung* the same for all Amish people everywhere?

No. Rules in the *Ordnung* can vary widely from affiliation to affiliation and can even vary somewhat from district to district within the same affiliation.

Does the *Ordnung* ever change?

Yes. As districts grow and divide into new ones, and as new technologies and issues arise, the *Ordnung* necessarily changes and adapts as well.

How and when do the rules get changed?

Passed along through an oral tradition, the *Ordnung* by necessity changes and evolves with every new issue that arises and every new technology that presents itself for consideration. Minor regulations are updated by church leaders as needed, but major decisions usually involve congregational input and often include debate in member meetings.

Regardless of how intensely various issues are debated, all matters of contention are laid to rest at the twice-yearly council meetings that precede the communion services. Once the group is at peace with one another and the rules, members reaffirm the commitment they made when they were first baptized to follow the *Ordnung*. In this way, they remain united as a people.

What do the Amish take into consideration when deciding on new rules or on making changes to old rules?

When deciding whether something should be allowed or modified, church leaders focus on key questions like these:

> *Will this force us to be more connected to the outside world?*
> *Will this create division in our families?*
> *Will this take us too far from home?*

For example, members of some Old Order communities do not have bicycles. Their thinking is that if one has a bicycle, he may take too much time away from home and family or venture into the outside world too fully. Thus, with an eye toward the what-ifs of a situation, a decision is made for the district and then becomes a part of its *Ordnung*.

Are all Amish required to follow the rules?

When a person is baptized into the Amish faith, he vows to obey God and the church for the rest of his life. This is an intentional, voluntary, adult act that requires a tremendous commitment and an act of submission that binds him under the rules of his district's *Ordnung*. Once this commitment has been made, any infraction of those rules is subject to church discipline, whether the infraction is minor (such as using forbidden technology) or major (such as committing adultery).

What happens if a person who has been baptized into the Amish faith breaks the rules?

The disciplinary process is careful and deliberate and usually begins with a reprimand from a church elder intended to bring reconciliation and repentance. If the disobedient member discontinues his infractions, confesses, and repents, then all is forgiven and he remains in good standing within the fold. If he continues in sin or gives up the sin but remains unrepentant, he is put on temporary probation.

What is the goal of this probation?

During the probationary period, repeated attempts are made to help him see the error of his ways. Elders, friends, and family will talk with him, pray for him, and remind him that he is not living in submission to church authority as he vowed to do when he was baptized. Many attempts are made toward reconciliation, and often this is enough to turn the most stubborn heart toward confession and repentance.

If the person still doesn't repent, what happens next?

At that point more drastic steps are taken. If the bishop recommends excommunication, the members will vote. If the vote passes, the person is excommunicated, or put under the "ban." In most districts, excommunication is followed by what the Amish call *Meidung*, or shunning. The severity of the shunning can vary widely from district to district. (See more about shunning in the following chapter.)

If an Amish person confesses and repents, do the Amish forgive and forget?

The Amish put great stress on forgiveness, especially the biblical principle of "Forgive, and you will be forgiven" found in verses such as Luke 6:37. They also feel that once a matter has been confessed and forgiven, it is also supposed to be forgotten. This new start with a clean slate makes for less baggage for all and can be the best way to move forward after an issue has been resolved.

Unfortunately, this can also create problems of recidivism. Applying this forgive-and-forget mentality to certain offenses can create much bigger problems, because without legal safeguards, even the most sincere of confessors can become repeat offenders.

Such was the case with the largest incidence of sexual assault in Amish American history. More than once, the rapists confessed and repented, only to commit the same atrocities soon thereafter.

Do the Amish ever report crimes to the police?

Yes, though more so nowadays than in the past. According to author David L. Weaver-Zercher, the Amish are more likely to involve police when they "feel they are in danger or when they're involved in a high-profile crime and have no other choice."[1]

Historically, the Amish have resisted involving law enforcement in all but the most serious of matters. Attitudes toward law enforcement have undergone a shift, however, in the wake of the massacre of Amish school students at Nickel Mines, Pennsylvania, in 2006. According to authors Donald B. Kraybill, Steven M. Nolt, and David L. Weaver-Zercher in their book *Amish Grace: How Forgiveness Transcended Tragedy*, many Amish were surprised by—and deeply grateful for—the outstanding efforts of the police during that difficult time. This has led many Amish to be more open to involving them in certain situations.[2] As Weaver-Zercher says, "Many [Amish] people gained an increased level of regard or comfort after what happened. There are often cases where Amish people become close to authorities, and in some ways those walls are lowered."[3]

With few exceptions, the Amish still do not believe pressing charges against another person, but instead prefer to solve disputes privately among themselves.

Are crimes ever perpetrated against the Amish by other Amish?

Though quite rare, this has happened. For example, there is the case of the Amish hair-cutting attacks in Ohio in 2011. Despite such offenses, the crime rate among the Amish is lower than that of the general population.

10

SHUNNING

What is shunning and when does it happen?

Shunning is a form of Amish church discipline reserved for church members who have committed serious infractions but refuse to confess and repent. As explained in the previous chapter, the disciplinary process in the Amish church starts with a reprimand from a church elder, followed by a temporary probation, followed by excommunication. In most districts, only after all of those steps have been taken—and if there is still no repentance—will the church then move on to the disciplinary step of shunning.

If someone is raised Amish but decides not to join the church, will they be shunned?

No. Those who have never been baptized into the church are not subject to excommunication or shunning. (See chapters 24 and 25, "*Rumspringa*" and "Baptism," for more information.)

Is shunning permanent?

It doesn't have to be. When a person is shunned, the door is always open to return to the fold as long as that person is willing to confess and repent. When one who has been shunned confesses to the church body with a contrite heart, all is forgiven, and the relationship is mended.

As one Amish man said, "Shunning is usually done with great reluctance and only when there is nothing else left to do. Upon repentance the relationship is restored, and what is in the past stays in the past."

What is shunning like?

Shunning is painful both for the one who is shunned and the ones who are doing the shunning, particularly the closest family members. In its strictest form, called *Streng Meidung,* members in good standing cannot dine at the same table with those who are shunned, nor can they accept rides or gifts from them or conduct business transactions. When one member of a married couple is shunned, the spouse in good standing may not sleep in the same bed or have marital relations. Conversation is sometimes allowed, but a definite line is drawn between the one who is under the ban and the rest of the community.

What purpose does shunning serve?

The primary goal of shunning is to bring about repentance. If that doesn't happen, then at least the secondary goal is accomplished: to keep the membership free from those who are not willing to follow the rules.

Isn't that a bit harsh?

The practice of shunning is one of the most well-known facets of Amish life. Unfortunately, it's also one of the most misunderstood. Though it's difficult for the non-Amish to comprehend, shunning is actually considered to be an act of love, one that is biblically based and done out of concern for the sinner.

It's important to remember that baptism and its accompanying commitment to honor the *Ordnung* and submit to the authority of the church are made voluntarily, not under duress, and as an adult, not as a child. As such, the candidate accepts from day one that any future infractions of the *Ordnung* will incur discipline.

Those who have been shunned and eventually repent and return to the fold are often grateful for the experience, saying it was difficult but in the end brought them closer to Christ and to the church. On the other hand, those who have been shunned but eventually leave the church often describe the experience as unspeakably cruel, an experience that will haunt them the rest of their lives.

What is the biblical basis for shunning?

In 1 Corinthians 5:11, the apostle Paul urged his brothers and sisters in Christ not to associate with "anyone who claims to be a brother or sister but is sexually immoral or greedy, an idolater or slanderer, a drunkard or swindler. Do not even eat with such people." In Romans 16:17, he says to "watch out for those who cause divisions and put obstacles in your way that are contrary to the teaching you have learned. Keep away from them."

11

HISTORY

When and where were the Amish formed?

First came the Anabaptist movement, which started in Switzerland in 1525 during the Protestant Reformation. One hero of the Anabaptist faith was Menno Simons, a Franciscan priest who left Catholicism to become an Anabaptist in 1536. Simons was a wise and influential leader, and his followers became known as the Mennonites. The Amish were a part of this group until 1693, when a leader in the Mennonite church named Jakob Ammann proposed a number of changes to the faith. Ammann's beliefs and practices eventually caused a split among the Mennonites, and those who followed Ammann became known as the Amish.

What were the changes to the Mennonite faith Jakob Ammann proposed?

Unlike the Mennonites, Ammann believed that communion should be held twice a year and should include foot washing, congregational regulations should be enforced to ensure doctrinal purity and spiritual discipline, and members who were excommunicated should be shunned.

What was the Anabaptist movement all about?

The roots of the Anabaptist movement lie with a small group of Christians who began to question certain practices of the Swiss church, in particular the deep intertwining of church and state, the church's financial dealings with the Swiss government, and infant baptism. The Anabaptists insisted that religious preference should be voluntary and free from government oversight.

Believing that the Bible stresses informed, adult baptism, these people eventually stopped baptizing their infants. Things came to a head in 1525, when this group was ordered by the city council of Zurich to do so. In response, the men of the group baptized one another instead. Because they had all been baptized previously as infants, they became known as "re-baptizers" or "Ana-baptists."

How did the church and state respond to these Anabaptists?

They were not pleased, to say the least. Attempts were made to squelch the movement, but despite numerous arrests and other government interference, the Anabaptists persisted.

Their movement gained strength, spreading so rapidly that within a year the Zurich city council passed an edict that made adult baptism a crime punishable by death. On January 5, 1527, an Anabaptist evangelist named Felix Manz was executed, making him one of the first Swiss Anabaptists to be martyred.

Were many early Anabaptists persecuted for their beliefs?

Yes. Between 1550 and 1625, more than 2500 Anabaptists were killed for their beliefs, often in horrific, tortuous ways. In response, they were forced to go underground and into rural areas to hide, with their meetings held in homes, barns, boats, and other private places. Some Mennonites immigrated to the Alsatian region of France to avoid persecution and compulsory military service.

Is this theme of persecution significant to the Amish?

Yes. The Amish focus heavily on their history and heritage, including past persecutions. The subject is often fodder for sermons, written works, and even casual conversation. Popular in many Amish homes is the *Martyrs Mirror*, a book with more than 1100 pages of text and artwork that depict the persecution suffered by many martyrs of the Christian faith.

When did the Amish first come to America?

The first American Amish settlements were begun in Berks County, Pennsylvania, in 1737 when a ship called the *Charming Nancy* sailed to America with 21 Amish families on board. More Amish followed in the years to come, and in the mid- to late-1700s, the early colonies of the present-day Lancaster County settlement were established. A second wave of Amish immigration began in 1815, when about 3000 adults surged into North America.

Did they settle in Pennsylvania as well?

Many of these second wave immigrants first came to Pennsylvania, but most of them moved on to other states, particularly Ohio, Illinois, Indiana, Iowa, and New York, as well as Ontario. By the mid-1800s, Amish settlements were dotted across the country.

Did the Amish church stay unified?

No. Sadly, internal disagreements and divisions would plague the Amish church for many years despite earnest attempts to resolve differences. Amish leaders struggled to find compromises and solutions in disputes about various Amish regulations. Groups that found themselves at impasses over nonnegotiable points sometimes split and formed new affiliations. The Old Order Amish were formed this way in 1865, followed by a number of other groups, such as the Beachy Amish in 1927 and the Andy Weaver Amish in 1952.

How were the Amish received by Americans?

In the early years, the Amish lifestyle and practices were not that different than those of other Americans, so they tended to blend in. But as the country changed and began adopting more industrialized/modern practices, the Amish began to stand out more and more. From the 1920s to the early 1970s, the Amish were viewed with suspicion and even hostility—especially during wartime, due to their pacifist stance.

In the mid-1970s, however, a new attitude about the Amish began to emerge as suspicion and contempt gave way to compassion and curiosity. Time passed, and ill feelings engendered during the World Wars faded into the background. As "diversity" and "tolerance" became American buzzwords, the Amish gained a new level of acceptance.

Did these problems with the non-Amish finally came to an end?

The days of blatant Amish persecution and ostracism may be gone, but now the Amish face a whole new set of problems as the pendulum has swung to the opposite extreme. With such a wide acceptance of and curiosity about the Amish, an entire branch of the tourism industry has developed, bringing with it overcrowding, intrusiveness, rising land costs, and outright exploitation. See chapter 29, "Tourism and the Media," for more information.

EXPANSION

How many baptized Amish adults are there?

Statistics differ, but most estimates come in between 120,000 and 125,000. (Add to that number unbaptized children and teens of Amish parents, and the total comes to almost 300,000 Amish currently living in the United States and Canada.)

Are the numbers of Amish increasing, declining, or staying the same?

Increasing. In fact, according to current statistics, the Amish population doubles about every 18 to 20 years. [1]

Why are their numbers increasing? Will this trend continue?

Future projections for Amish population growth vary widely, but most experts say this increase shows no signs of slowing anytime soon. Growth is propelled by two factors: the high birth rate and the high retention rate. About 85 percent of those raised in Amish homes decide to join the Amish church once they are grown.

How many children are in the average Amish family?

Statistics differ, so an exact figure is hard to come by. Experts quote averages as low as five and as high as nine, but the general consensus seems to fall at around seven.

Where do the Amish live?

Amish communities are in 30 U.S. states and one Canadian province. As of July 2012, the five most Amish-populated states, in order, were:

1. Ohio
2. Pennsylvania
3. Indiana
4. Wisconsin
5. New York[2]

What happens if an Amish person wants to move away? Are they allowed to leave?

Yes. Migrating Amish may move away to join an established settlement elsewhere or start a new settlement from scratch.

Why do some Amish choose to move away and start new settlements elsewhere?

The number one reason the Amish might leave an established community and head to a new area is to find available and affordable farmland. This is especially the case in Lancaster County, where family farms have been divided and subdivided over the years and most have reached their limits and can be divided no further. Even when new land is available there, prices have climbed so high that young farmers cannot afford to purchase large tracts.

Other reasons Amish families will migrate out of an established settlement include:

- to get away from excessive tourism
- to avoid conflicts over zoning laws and other municipal issues
- to escape areas with particularly weak economies and poor job markets
- to sever relations with a particular church district and start anew elsewhere

How do the Amish decide where to establish new settlements?

When choosing a location for a new settlement, the Amish consider criteria such as:

- reasonable land prices
- fertile soil and good farming climate
- occupational opportunities
- proximity to relatives or other Amish communities
- proximity to similar districts within an affiliation
- non-Amish neighbors' acceptance of the Amish and their ways

Do any Amish live in Europe?

No. In various European countries, settlements of what is known as the "Beachy Amish" exist, but the Beachy Amish are actually closer in practice to Mennonites than what we think of as Amish. The Beachy Amish wear Plain clothing and put some limits on formal education, but unlike the Old Order Amish, the Beachy Amish worship in church buildings, conduct a full range of theological education classes, and are involved in missions. They also allow a wider use of technology, including cars, electricity, and the Internet.

No Old Order Amish settlements have been in Europe since the late 1930s.

Part Two:
LIFESTYLE

I was astounded at the sheer quantity of food that was heaped upon platters on the table: pork chops in sauerkraut, homemade bread, noodles in butter, and a variety of vegetables that the family had likely grown and canned themselves. After a silent prayer, everyone dug in, and even the women scooped up generous portions of butter for their bread.

The meal passed so pleasantly that about halfway through I simply allowed myself to sit there and take it all in. How could I have forgotten what it was like to be in an Amish kitchen and listen to the gentle banter, the politeness of the children, the sweet teasing of the husband and wife?

—Excerpted from *Shadows of Lancaster County*
by Mindy Starns Clark

AMISH LIFE

What is a typical day for an Amish man?

For Amish farmers, weekdays begin quite early. For most of the day, they can usually be found working with their crops out in the fields or in the barn, milking the cows and/or caring for the animals. Time may also be spent with the children and guiding them as they learn various farm-related chores, chopping wood, making household repairs, and more. All three meals are eaten at home. Evenings are quiet, most often spent reading or playing games or simply visiting with friends and family.

How about for men who aren't farmers?

As farmland grows scarce in crowded settlements, more and more Amish men are moving into the workplace, often at factories in positions of manual labor. Though this allows them to earn a living wage, the Amish see this type of situation as less than ideal because it keeps fathers from the home for far too long each day, and because it places them too fully in the midst of non-Amish environments.

Alternatively, many nonfarming Amish operate their own businesses, both the kind that serve other Amish, such as buggy shops, and those that cater to a non-Amish clientele, such as furniture making. The more that Amish craftsmanship grows in popularity, the greater the number of Amish-owned businesses that continue to pop up.

According to author Erik Wesner in *Success Made Simple: An Inside Look at Why Amish Businesses Thrive*, entrepreneurship provides Amish men with a viable alternative to farming. As he says, "Amish forefathers sowed their acres with the ultimate aim of perpetuating family and faith. Amish entrepreneurs today cultivate their businesses with similar ambitions in mind."[1]

Because of this, Wesner contends, whether a man works in or out of the home, breakfast always "takes place at the table, bookended by prayer—rather than on TV trays, or wolfed down on the way out the door. Amish believe there should always be time for sit-down meal; it's not only family time but a chance to rest and recharge."[2]

What is a typical day for an Amish woman?

The typical Amish wife rises before dawn and labors all day long, especially if her husband works away from the home. She prepares three full meals a day, cares for the children, sews all of the clothing for her family, does the laundry (most often with a wringer washing machine and no dryer), grows a "kitchen garden," cans fruits and vegetables, does the grocery shopping, teaches the children their various household chores and responsibilities, keeps the home clean, handwashes the dishes, and more.

With all of that work to do every day, are these women miserable?

According to authors Merle and Phyllis Good in their book *20 Most Asked Questions about the Amish and Mennonites*, "An Old Order woman is a worker, a child-bearer, and a companion to her husband, family, and neighbors."[3] Though hardworking, Amish women are far less isolated than the average American housewife, and as their families grow they have more and more hands to share the load. Thus, most Amish women would likely describe themselves as content rather than miserable.

Certainly, there are those who feel overburdened and exhausted. But as authors Good and Good say, "When a woman's ambitions fit her society's framework, and her peers' experiences parallel her own, she is less likely to be restless and dissatisfied."[4]

What is a typical day for an Amish child?

Depending on age, an Amish child's day usually consists of school, chores, and playtime. Comparatively speaking, Amish children typically spend more time in the company of their parents, interact more fully with older generations, and have more responsibilities around the house and farm than their non-Amish counterparts. As authors Good and Good say, "It is in the fields and the kitchen that the Old Order family is solidified."[5]

Can you tell the difference between an Amish home and a non-Amish home just by looking?

From the outside, there are usually some "giveaways" to indicate an Amish family lives inside. No electric lines run to the house, and the window treatments are extremely plain, such as green pull-down shades or simple white curtains. You might also catch the occasional glimpse of a horse and buggy in the driveway or Amish garments hanging from the clothesline. Finally, in some communities the presence of cockscomb flowers outside indicates that an Amish family lives inside.

Amish farmhouses also often have a typical "look," as they tend to be large and rambling thanks to additional rooms and small apartments added on as families expand and/or members grow old. Even at homes with indoor plumbing, there may be outhouses in the yard as well.

What are Amish homes like on the inside?

Amish homes differ from non-Amish homes in that they have no televisions, stereos, computers, telephones, or other modern technological devices. They are also decidedly plain, with an emphasis on simplicity and thrift. Much of the furniture is handmade, of wood, using fine Amish craftsmanship. Decorations are primarily functional; for example, artwork hanging on the wall will likely include a calendar or weather chart.

Otherwise, the way things look on the inside can vary greatly depending on the district's *Ordnung*. Homes in less conservative districts can appear quite modern at first glance. Kitchens will have refrigerators, stoves, and small appliances; bathrooms will feature sinks and toilets with plumbing; and there will be lighting and heat throughout the home. (As you will see in chapter 18, "Technology," the Amish do not use electricity but have adapted many household devices so that they work with other energy sources, such as coal, compressed air, diesel, gasoline, kerosene, propane, water, wind, and wood.)

Homes in more conservative districts may be less ornamented, with few personal touches, sparse furnishings, and only the most rudimentary of appliances.

Conservative or not, many Amish homes feature a large living room or other common area where the family can gather together in the evenings. Because church services are held in homes rather than in church buildings, sliding walls and doors are often built in so that they can expand these rooms even further to accommodate entire congregations.

Do the Amish shop in non-Amish stores?

Yes. The average Amish home has a "kitchen garden," where fresh produce is grown for the family to eat. But for additional food items—as well as numerous other types of consumer goods—the Amish patronize a variety of non-Amish stores, from discount chains to hardware stores to dry goods stores and more. They also shop via mail order.

Do the Amish use banks and money?

Yes. The Amish use banks for checking accounts, savings accounts, loans, and sometimes even credit cards. When given the choice, they prefer to deal with small, local banks rather than large conglomerates.

In Amish-heavy regions such as Lancaster County, it is not unusual to see a horse and buggy in line for a bank's drive-through window.

—— IN THEIR OWN WORDS ——

Sometimes we do agree to look the other way.
For lesser things that are frowned upon, like
smoking or hanging up decorations, well, those
things are just kind of "tolerated," so to speak,
in the interest of community harmony.

Do the Amish drink?

There is no overall Amish rule against drinking. Instead, the practice varies by district. Where permitted, moderation is emphasized.

While alcohol consumption is not unheard of among the Amish, it is not the norm. As author Erik Wesner says, you'll be "a lot more likely to catch an Amish fella with a cold can of Dew, a piping-hot cup of coffee, or a tin of straight-from-the-udder raw milk than a cool Bud."[6]

Do the Amish smoke?

Pipe and cigar smoking are somewhat acceptable, but cigarette smoking among the Amish is rare.

A few Amish communities consider tobacco to be an acceptable crop, primarily because it is labor-intensive and can be grown and harvested without need for modern, technological equipment.

Do the Amish use guns?

Yes. The Amish generally have no bans against hunting and may own firearms. Their guns are never meant to be used as weapons against humans, however, not even in self-defense. The Amish believe in non-resistance and will not bear arms against other people.

14

FOOD

What sorts of foods do the Amish eat?

Derived from a Pennsylvania Dutch tradition, the food the Amish prefer is simple and satisfying. Meals usually feature fruits and vegetables grown in their own gardens (either fresh picked or that which was canned while in season) and include much of what we non-Amish think of as comfort food, such as potato dishes, breads, noodles, and pies. Because the Amish live a physically demanding lifestyle, they do not generally worry too much about things like fat content or calorie counts.

What beverages do the Amish like to drink?

Coffee—usually black—is heavily consumed among the Amish. Other popular beverages include water, juice, tea, soda, and milk.

Do the Amish grow their own fruits and vegetables?

Yes. The Amish grow much of their own food, and they put up fruits and vegetables. A good harvest, well canned, will carry a household through many months.

Where do they get the rest of their food?

Besides the produce grown in their gardens, the Amish may also:

- have laying hens for eggs
- keep cows for milk and other dairy products
- raise chickens, pigs, and other livestock for slaughter
- hunt wild game

Additionally, they buy food at supermarkets, discount chains, big box stores, and other regular grocery outlets, just as the non-Amish do.

Do the Amish ever eat in restaurants?

Yes, at least in the less conservative districts. Though it would be considered wasteful and worldly to dine out often or lavishly, an occasional trip to a moderately priced restaurant has become a common occurrence in many Amish communities.

What are some favorite Amish dishes?

One well-known Amish treat is shoofly pie, a dessert made with molasses, flour, and brown sugar that is a daily staple in many Amish homes. Other Amish favorites include:

- scrapple—a meat-based product made with pork, corn meal, and flour which is congealed into a loaf and then sliced and pan fried
- chow chow—a mixture of pickled vegetables
- snitz/schnitz/shitz pie—a sweet pie made from dried apples
- fry pie—a pocket of fried pie crust filled with various flavors of pie filling
- whoopie pie—sweet creme sandwiched between two small chocolate cakes

Can you share a good Amish recipe?

Sure! Here's one of my favorites.

AMISH CHEESY POTATOES

    2 lbs. potatoes
    ½ cup butter
    1 can cream of mushroom soup
    1 pint sour cream
    2 cups Velveeta cheese, cut into cubes
    ½ teaspoon garlic powder

¼ teaspoon pepper
¼ teaspoon salt
2 cups crushed cornflakes

Peel and slice potatoes and then place them in water in a large pot. Boil until almost done and then drain. In a medium saucepan, combine butter, soup, sour cream, cheese, and seasonings; stir until butter and cheese are melted and all ingredients are combined. Gently fold the cheese mixture into the potatoes. In a casserole dish, layer the cheesy potato mixture with the crushed cereal, starting with a layer of potatoes and ending with a light sprinkling of cereal. Bake at 350 degrees until bubbly and golden brown, about 45 minutes.

For other delicious Amish recipes, I recommend *The Homestyle Amish Kitchen Cookbook* by Georgia Varozza and *The Amish Family Cookbook* by Jerry and Tina Eicher.

15

HEALTH

Do the Amish go to doctors or use hospitals?

Yes. Though many Amish are likely to treat ailments with natural or traditional approaches first, they generally have no problem with seeking modern medical care when the situation warrants.

Why not go to the doctor right away?

For financial or holistic reasons, the Amish may be less likely to seek out professional help than the non-Amish, especially with minor ailments or injuries. Generally, the more conservative the district, the more likely they are to rely on their own home treatments first, using doctors and hospitals only as a last resort.

Do they believe in getting vaccinated?

Generally speaking, yes, though some abstain for religious reasons or because of safety concerns—particularly from vaccinations associated with autism.

Do they practice family planning?

Most Amish couples want many children, so family planning is not usually necessary. When desired, however, it depends on the district. Some districts discourage or prohibit the use of birth control, while others consider it a private matter left to the discretion of husband and wife.

Do the Amish have their babies at home or in the hospital?

Both, and at birthing centers too. Though a number of Amish women give birth in hospitals, many opt for home births or birthing centers instead. They do so for several reasons:

- cost—home births are much less expensive than hospital births
- comfort—many women find the home environment far less stressful for labor and delivery
- proximity—most women would rather be surrounded by their own family members than by a staff of paid medical workers

Depending on the region, hospital and home births may be attended by a physician, nurse-midwife, or midwife. Generally, the more conservative the district, the more likely they are to use midwives and home births.

Do the Amish use health insurance?

No. Because of their belief in remaining separate from the world, the Amish generally do not use health insurance. Most medical expenses are simply paid out of pocket by the family involved.

For large expenses a family cannot afford, costs are usually covered by their community. The Amish believe this binds them together and forces them to depend more heavily on one another.

Is it true they prefer to seek treatment outside of the United States?

No, but some Amish will travel to other countries, primarily Mexico, to save money on more exorbitant medical treatments.

Is there such a thing as an Amish doctor or an Amish hospital?

The Amish end their formal educations at the eighth grade and professional degrees are not pursued, so the Amish would not be adequately schooled to become a doctor. There are, however, non-Amish doctors who specialize in treating the Amish.

There are also hospitals and other facilities with a decidedly Amish clientele, such as the Clinic for Special Children in Strasburg, Pennsylvania; the Mount Eaton Care Center in Mount Eaton, Ohio; and the Pomerene Hospital in Millersburg, Ohio.

What about mental health? Do the Amish ever seek treatment from psychiatrists, psychologists, and or family therapists? Do they ever seek professional counseling?

Yes. If necessary, most Amish will seek mental health care, though the counseling process can be hindered if the medical professional involved is not familiar with a Plain lifestyle—or, worse, if he sees it as part of the problem. Thus, many Amish who need mental health services seek out Mennonite-based facilities such as at Philhaven in Mount Gretna, Pennsylvania. There they can receive services from professionals who are experienced with—and respectful of—the Plain lifestyle.

Why do the Amish seem to deal with more than their fair share of genetic disorders?

Unfortunately, the Amish suffer from what is known as the "founder effect," which means they can trace their genetic roots back to a small set of common ancestors. (This can also be found in other culturally isolated religious groups, such as the Ashkenazi Jews, as well as in communities that are geographically isolated, such as the island-based populations of Iceland and Easter Island.)

Through many generations of genetic intermixing, mutations of DNA have caused the proliferation of rare disorders among the Amish—for example, dwarfism and maple syrup urine disease—that tend to be much more common for them than in the wider population. They also have a greater incidence of rare blood types.

The flip side of this problematic situation is that DNA researchers have been able to study the Amish to glean information from their genes, information that can help to identify and treat a host of rare and common genetically influenced disorders (such as diabetes) that affect both the Amish and the population at large.

Are the Amish willing to participate in medical research?

Yes. For the most part, the Amish have been extremely cooperative with researchers, allowing blood draws for scientific study. In turn, researchers at places like the Clinic for Special Children in Lancaster County work closely with the Amish to help treat and prevent the rare disorders that occur with such a high frequency among them.

16

CLOTHING AND GROOMING

Why do the Amish dress the way they do?

The Amish way of dressing and grooming is highly regulated, primarily for two reasons: as a demonstration of submission to authority and to provide a visible public symbol of group identity. Outsiders who know nothing about the ways and values of the Amish can easily recognize them because of how they dress.

Why is it so important to them to conform to a set of rules regarding clothes?

Clothing is just one more area in which the Amish desire to be more Christlike. They believe the practice of regulated dressing emphasizes the following virtues:

- *Humility*: Dressing alike provides less opportunity for vanity.
- *Submission*: Following the clothing rules of the district demonstrates obedience to God, to the group, and to history.
- *Denial of self*: Dressing alike prevents individuality and pride.
- *Simplicity*: Limiting clothing choices saves time and effort.
- *Modesty*: Prescribed styles guarantee propriety.
- *Thrift*: Making clothes, especially from limited fabric and pattern choices, saves money, as does the lack of jewelry and accessories.

What sorts of clothing regulations are there?

In general, the district's *Ordnung* addresses matters of head coverings, hairstyles, facial hair for men, clothing choices for males and females, and footwear. There are also clothing and grooming differences between those who are married and unmarried.

Are all Amish under the exact same clothing rules?

Specific rules vary between districts and affiliations, but members of the same district will dress and groom themselves by the same set of rules. Thus, to someone in the know, just a simple difference in hat brim width can clearly identify the specific district to which the hat's owner belongs.

What clothing elements do various Amish districts have in common?

Though specifics can vary from district to district, all Amish clothing is modest, loose fitting, and of a predetermined style and choice of colors. Clothing worn to church differs somewhat from that worn during the week. In some districts, buttons, collars, and lapels are taboo because they are too closely associated with military uniforms.

Head coverings are worn every day by men, women, and teens. Children wear head coverings in church and at school, though not always in more casual settings, depending on district rules.

What kinds of shoes do the Amish wear?

Many Amish, both young and old, enjoy going barefoot much of the time. Shoes, when worn, may be lace-ups, slip-ons, or sneakers, depending on district rules, and are almost always dark.

Amish women often go barefoot at home. When shoes are worn, they are usually paired with dark stockings.

What does a typical Amish man's outfit consist of?

For everyday wear, Amish men usually sport dark broadfall trousers held up by suspenders. In the interest of modesty, suspenders allow for a looser fit, and in the interest of humility, they supplant belt buckles, which are considered fancy.

Shirts are in prescribed colors only, and though Old Order Amish and other conservative groups do not allow plaids or stripes, some less conservative sects may.

Men usually wear banded straw hats for work and chores, with the width of the brim and the height of the crown determined by district rules. In settings other than work, such as going into town or gathering for church, they sport black felt hats of a specified height and brim width.

What are these felt hats like?

They are exceptionally well crafted and expensive, which is why most boys instead wear lower-quality, less costly versions. When a young man joins the church, usually in his late teens or early twenties, he is often given a "real" hat, one he will tend carefully and use for many years.

What colors do the Amish wear?

Approved colors vary from district to district, but they are most often ones found in nature, such as blue, green, brown, and maroon.

How about fabrics? Do they have to be natural, such as cotton or wool?

Not usually. Most districts allow the use of modern synthetic fabrics as long as they aren't "fancy" (for example, no velvet, silk, or satin) and are in the permitted range of colors.

Do the Amish dress differently for church?

Women's clothing is generally the same every day of the week. The men dress differently on Sundays, with black wool or felt hats along with black dress shoes, black suits, and white shirts. Suits include broadfall pants with suspenders, vests fastened with hooks and eyes, and coats, which may or may not have buttons or lapels, depending on district rules.

What are the rules about men's hairstyles and facial hair?

Hair is worn blunt cut in a uniform style, usually no longer than collar length.

Men shave their faces until they marry, at which point they stop shaving their beard, though they continue to shave their mustaches. In general, beards are not to be trimmed or neatened.

Why can they have beards but not mustaches?

Like buttons and lapels, mustaches are avoided because they are associated with the military.

Do they have rules about women's hairstyles?

Yes. In deference to 1 Corinthians 11:2-16, Amish women never cut their hair but instead allow it to grow. They consider a woman's hair to be her glory, which she shares only with her husband in private. Otherwise, Amish women part their hair in the middle, pull it tightly back, and fasten it into a bun or braid. Prayer coverings are worn over the hair. In general, the less conservative a district, the smaller the female's head covering.

What does a typical Amish woman's outfit consist of?

Women sport calf- to ankle-length full-skirted dresses. Over these go aprons and capes, usually black. Capes are made from a wide piece of fabric that is crossed in the front and comes to a point in the back. Straight pins are usually used in lieu of buttons to fasten the cape at the waist in front and back.

Women wear prayer coverings (also called *kapps*) on their heads. Depending on district and marital status, these coverings may be white or black. They often cover the ears at least partially and have strings that may or may not be tied, also depending on district rules. In winter, a warmer bonnet of an approved design may be worn over the prayer cap.

Why do they wear prayer coverings?

Prayer coverings are worn in deference to a number of biblical passages; for example, 1 Corinthians 11:5, which says a woman "who prays or prophesies with her head uncovered dishonors her head." Amish women wear their *kapps* from morning to night, both in and out of the home.

What's the difference between a *kapp* and a bonnet?

Bonnets are sometimes added in certain situations, both for warmth and protection from the elements and also as a public symbol of modesty and submission. Bonnets are worn in addition to *kapps*, not instead of them.

Where do the Amish get their clothes?

Amish women sew most of the clothes for their family, though some stores do sell ready-made clothing. As girls grow up, they are taught to sew, and by their teenage years they may be skilled enough to help outfit the entire family.

Are there rules about underclothes? Do they make their own?

Most Amish wear plain-looking store-bought undergarments, though there are some conservative districts where underwear is handmade and bras are not allowed.

Can Amish women wear makeup? How about jewelry?

No. Neither makeup nor jewelry is worn, not even wedding rings.

What do Amish children wear?

Girls usually wear solid-color jumpers in approved colors, topped by loose, pinafore-style white or black aprons.

For school, play, or chores, boys wear broadfall pants with suspenders and shirts in approved colors along with banded straw hats. For church, they wear black suits similar in style to those worn by the adults, along with black felt hats.

Baby boys are generally clothed in dresses until they are potty trained.

What do the Amish use for diapers?

Many Amish women sew their own cloth diapers, though disposables may be used as well, especially when away from the home.

Where do they keep their clothes?

When not being worn, men's felt hats are often kept in hat presses. In many Amish homes, clothing is stored on pegs along the wall.

This illustration shows the clothes and hats in the boys' room of an Amish home. The dress hanging second from the left is for the male toddler of the room, who will wear dresses until he is potty trained, at which point he will graduate to the pants-and-shirt attire of his older brothers.

17

LANGUAGE

What languages do the Amish speak?

Amish life involves three different languages: Pennsylvania Dutch, English, and High German.

What is Pennsylvania Dutch?

A common misconception about Pennsylvania Dutch is that it is a variant of the Dutch language. This isn't true. The German word for "German" is *Deutsch*, which sounds a lot like "Dutch," and the theory holds that over the years, the term for Pennsylvania German, or Pennsylvania *Deutsch*, began to be pronounced Pennsylvania Dutch.

The language is based on a Palatine dialect that was brought to America from Germany in the 1700s, primarily by a mass influx of Lutherans and German Reformed Church members searching for religious freedom. Once here, their dialect began to mix with other dialects and with the English of the colonists, evolving into what eventually became known as Pennsylvania Dutch. Today, though the language's grammatical structures are still based on Palatine German, about 5 to 10 percent of the vocabulary comes from the English language.

Where is Pennsylvania Dutch spoken?

Pennsylvania Dutch is the primary language of the Amish, spoken at home, in sermons at church, and among other Amish. Though other religious groups also spoke this German-derived American language in the past, the Amish and the Old Order Mennonites maintain it to the present day. (An exception to this is in Indiana, where a few

Amish communities use a Swiss dialect for their primary language rather than Pennsylvania Dutch.)

What does it sound like?

To hear live recordings of Pennsylvania Dutch being spoken, visit www.amishfaqs.com/helpful.php and click on the link near the bottom of the page.

Where do they speak English?

For the Amish, English is the language of commerce, literacy, and the outside world. Teens and adults are fluent in English and use the language when speaking with non-Amish friends, conducting business outside of the community, and functioning in other non-Amish settings.

Most children grow up knowing only Pennsylvania Dutch but are then taught to speak, read, and write English in school.

Why aren't small children taught to speak English from the very beginning?

Limiting their knowledge to Pennsylvania Dutch helps insulate and protect young ones from outside influences for the first five to seven years of their lives.

Where is High German spoken?

High German is the language of respect for God and heritage and is used in Amish worship services and spiritual texts. Most Amish become familiar with the language not through formal instruction but rather from years of exposure during Sunday worship and when reading the classics of the Amish faith that are in High German. These include:

- The *Ausbund*, or Amish hymnal, which was first published in 1564. Many of its songs were written by martyrs of the faith in the sixteenth century. It is the oldest Christian songbook in continuous use.

- *Die Ernsthafte Christenpflicht,* a prayer book used in many Amish households.
- The Luther Bible.

Do the Amish speak English with an accent?

Some do, some don't. But even for those Amish who speak English without any telltale accent, there are some giveaways when they talk, particularly among those who do not converse often with outsiders. Certain words and terms receive unusual pronunciations and uniquely Amish phraseology.

Is their sentence construction old-fashioned and formal?

No. Contrary to how the Amish are often portrayed in the media, they do not use archaic terms such as "thee" and "thou" when speaking English.

18

TECHNOLOGY

Do the Amish reject technology?

No. But they are selective about which technological devices and innovations they consider to be acceptable. Because of this, some types of technology are permitted, and some are not. For example, an Amish district might allow generator-powered sewing machines but forbid generator-powered clothes dryers.

Do they own cars?

No.

Do they consider technology to be evil or wrong?

No, but they do believe that if left unchecked, certain technologies can destroy the Amish way of life by undermining its traditions, bringing inappropriate value systems into homes, and ultimately breaking communities and families apart. This is why they are so selective about which devices and innovations they will and will not use.

Their rules seem so arbitrary—contradictory, even. For example, why do the Amish not own or drive cars, yet they will ride in vehicles driven by others? Why do they not use electricity, yet they will use other forms of power, such as propane and gasoline? Why won't they have a phone in the house but put one in the barn?

To make sense of these questions, it's important to consider the Amish value system and how it applies to technology, as shown:

- *Humility*: A lack of fancy electronic devices provides less opportunity for pride.

- *Submission*: Following the technology rules of the order demonstrates obedience to God, to the group, and to history.
- *Community*: Staying off the grid prevents dependence on the outside world.
- *Simplicity*: Life without computers, e-mail, or other forms of electronic interruption is more peaceful.
- *Thrift*: A low-tech life prevents excessive phone bills, car insurance premiums, cable TV charges, Internet costs, music download fees, and so on.
- *Family*: Owning and driving one's own car provides too many opportunities for temptation and allows one to roam too far from home.

Also, it's important to remember that external technologies such as cars are used only with intention, never capriciously. An Amish person would never hire a car and driver for a mere joy ride. The ride in the car needs to come from necessity; for example, a doctor's appointment or to visit a distant relative.

Rules that seem contradictory usually relate to the overriding goal of being masters over technology rather than slaves to it. Any non-Amish person who has ever felt a prisoner to a constantly ringing phone or a full e-mail inbox can surely understand that concept.

Who and/or what determines if a technology fits into the value system?

As explained in chapter 9, "Rules," when a new technology becomes available to a district, church leaders will evaluate its potential for causing harm to Amish life and values and then decide whether to allow it. No technology, regardless of how labor-saving it may be, is permissible if the leaders determine it will be spiritually detrimental to the community.

What are some examples of acceptable technological devices?

Though the rules vary widely from district to district, many technological items are allowed in Amish homes and farms, such as calculators, flashlights, manual typewriters, gas grills, chain saws, and inline skates. Some districts permit gas-powered lawn mowers and even weed whackers.

Is it true the Amish don't have electricity?
Yes. Most Amish do not have electricity in their homes.

Do they use other forms of power?

Yes. In many Amish homes and farms, certain items are allowed as long as they have been adapted to work with non-electric fuel sources, such as propane or batteries. These would include refrigerators, lights, shop tools, fans, copy machines, sewing machines, smoke alarms, some farm equipment, hot water heaters, washing machines, and more.

What do they use to power these adapted devices?
Not all districts allow all types of power, but the Amish have found remarkably ingenious ways to make their lives easier using permissible power sources instead of hooking into the grid, for example:

- lanterns and lamps powered by kerosene, naphtha, gasoline, or propane
- stoves powered by wood, kerosene, bottled gas, or propane
- refrigerators powered by kerosene or propane
- small appliances powered by compressed air
- plumbing powered by wind, water, gas, diesel, compressed air, or gravity
- water heaters powered by wood, coal, kerosene, or bottled gas
- household heaters powered by wood, propane, or natural gas
- washing machines powered by compressed air or gasoline

Is high-tech farm equipment also adapted?

Frequently, yes. Tractors often must be changed so that they can be used for off-road use only, lest they provide the opportunity to go too far from home. This usually means steel tires rather than rubber. In many communities, tractors are not used in the fields at all but instead may only be used inside or near the barn as sources for high-powered needs such as blowing silage to the top of silos, powering feed grinders and hydraulic systems, pumping liquid manure, and so on.

In most cases, hay balers can be used in the fields as long as they are pulled by horses rather than self-propelled.

What about digital technology?

Digital technology is one of the greatest current technological threats to the Amish way of life. As more and more Amish leave farming behind and take up manufacturing and other jobs, they are exposed to computers, cell phones, and the Internet. To further complicate matters, many Amish-owned businesses, including farms, have felt compelled to enter the computer and cell-phone age as well.

If this type of technology is such a problem, why don't the Amish just ban digital devices altogether?

When the success or failure of a business depends on a device, leaders hesitate to draw the line and say it cannot be used—at least, not hastily and without an enormous amount of thought and debate first. How these problems will be handled remains to be seen.

Have the Amish ever faced anything like this in the past?

To an extent. For example, the use of tractors on farms has been problematic for years. Starting as far back as the 1920s, leaders have faced tractor-related conundrums that have required much thought and careful decision making all along the way, especially with the release of each new type of tractor technology that has come along.

Isn't there a big difference between a tractor and a laptop?

Yes. Unfortunately for the Amish, digital technology development races along at a speed far greater than that of mechanical tractor development. Until districts draw hard-and-fast rules for or against various types of digital technology, more and more Amish are gaining exposure to and experience with them.

What about cell phones?

Cell phones are a huge issue as they are used both by parents in the workplace and often by teens prior to baptism. One isn't likely to see a cell phone at an Amish dinner table anytime soon, but many are kept tucked away to be used in more private moments.

One Amish mother explains that she wouldn't have a problem with her teens owning cell phones (as long as they didn't use them while inside the home), but she *is* concerned about the Internet access that her children would get through those cell phones.

Until a final decision is made, this quiet infiltration is likely to continue. On a recent trip to Lancaster County, I personally saw a sight that made me do a double take: an Amish youth, relaxing on a trampoline in his front yard, busily texting away with his thumbs just like any other American teenager.

Are there rules about landline telephones?

Yes. Telephones are not installed in Amish homes, for various reasons, but primarily because:

- Landlines form a connection with the world.

- Telephones can disrupt the peacefulness of home life.

- Unnecessary telephone conversations can lead to gossip.

- Telephone use eliminates the need for many face-to-face interactions with other members of the community.

Because of the necessity of this type of communication in certain situations (emergencies, long-distance relationships that require an immediate response to a need or question, and necessary interaction with the non-Amish), shared telephones are used in most districts. Such phones will often be installed in barns or in "phone shanties" and are used by the surrounding families as needed.

—— IN THEIR OWN WORDS ——

I cannot imagine what it would be like if
we had a telephone in the house. Even with
the phone out in the barn, our teenager already
calls her friends two or three times a week!

What's a phone shanty?

A phone shanty is a little building, not connected to any home, that contains a telephone and phone book. Shanties are located between neighboring farms so they can be used by more than one family. Calls are recorded in a notebook or "call log" and bills settled at the end of each month.

Do these shared phones have voice mail or answering machines?

Usually they do, though messages may be checked and calls returned somewhat infrequently.

What about cameras? Is it true that the Amish don't want to be photographed?

Yes, that is true. Most Amish do not own cameras or take photographs, though this has nothing to do with restrictions on technology. Instead, they believe photographs are biblically prohibited by Exodus 20:4, which says, "You shall not make for yourself an image in the form of anything in heaven above or on the earth beneath or in the waters below."

19

TRANSPORTATION

Why don't the Amish use cars?
The Amish do not drive or own cars for several reasons, including:

- *Humility*: A lack of expensive, fancy cars provides less opportunity for pride.
- *Submission*: Following the transportation rules demonstrates obedience to God, to the group, and to history.
- *Community*: When travel is limited, everyone stays closer together and depends on one another.
- *Thrift*: Not owning a car eliminates loan payments, insurance, repairs, maintenance, and gasoline.
- *Family*: Owning and driving one's own car provides too many opportunities for tempta-tion and allows one to roam too far from home.
- *Separation*: Their distinctive form of transportation provides a visible symbol of their separation from the world.

But why horse and buggy? Aren't there easier ways to get around?
The Amish say that riding in a horse and buggy keeps life at a slower pace and allows more time to look around and notice the beauty of their surroundings.

Are there rules related to Amish buggies?

Yes. Almost all aspects of buggies are regulated by the district in one way or another. These rules deal with color (black, gray, brown, white, or yellow), lights (battery powered or kerosene), style (covered or uncovered), mirrors, blinkers, safety markings, and more.

Why do I see Amish using different types of buggies?

Different situations call for different types of buggies. Some common buggy types include:

- family wagons, which have room for parents and children inside and windows in the back
- courting buggies, which have a single seat for two and no top, allowing unmarried couples to ride together without too much privacy
- bench wagons, which transport the benches used for Sunday services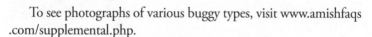
- minister's wagons, which are like family buggies but without the storm front
- pickup wagons or market wagons, which have an open back
- spring wagons, which have room for two or three people and no top

To see photographs of various buggy types, visit www.amishfaqs.com/supplemental.php.

What are the orange triangles on the backs of their buggies?

Over the years, as roads have become more congested with cars, the Amish have had to adopt certain safety equipment on their buggies, such as reflective triangles or tape, turn indicators, mirrors, and lights. Church leaders are sometimes at odds with municipal authorities over these items because they feel they are flashy and encourage pride.

However, the Amish have slowly begun to compromise for the sake of the greater good and the safety of their members.

What if they are in a hurry or have to go farther away than a horse and buggy can take them? Do they have other options?

Yes. Most districts will use public transportation, though some have restrictions against air travel. Bicycles are used by some groups but not others. In Lancaster County, the simplest way to get around is on a scooter.

Many Amish communities also have "Amish taxis." These are cars with non-Amish drivers hired by the Amish to take them to work, appointments, and trips. In most cases, Amish taxis are not to be used to get to church.

Children on the farm enjoy riding in pony carts. These are like open-top buggies in miniature, pulled by ponies. Children learn to drive their pony carts at a very young age, and if their ponies are shod, they may even take them out on the road.

OCCUPATIONS

Do the Amish have a preferred or primary occupation?

Yes. The primary occupation of the Amish has always been farming. Unfortunately, in some of the more population-dense settlements such as Lancaster County, Pennsylvania, rising land costs and decreased availability of farmland are making it much more difficult for younger Amish to continue this tradition.

Why farming?

In the early days of the Anabaptist movement, many fled into the countryside to avoid persecution. There they learned farming skills, which they later brought to America.

The Amish believe that, according to Scripture, farming is a sacred lifestyle and a way to connect closely with God. Farmwork helps ingrain many Amish values, including a strong work ethic, patience, and simplicity.

Are their farms big? What sorts of crops do they usually grow?

The average Amish farm in Lancaster County has about 70 acres, and the crops commonly include corn, tobacco, alfalfa, or various grains. Dairy farms are also common.

Besides farming, what other occupations do the Amish hold?

They work in other trades, factories, restaurants, retail establishments, farmers' markets, and so on. Amish women may also work as housecleaners.

Is entrepreneurship common among the Amish?

Yes. The Amish are starting up their own home-based businesses in record numbers.

Are these home-based businesses successful?

Frequently, they are. Glenn Rifkin gives this report in the *New York Times*:

> The businesses, which favor such Amish skills as furniture-making, quilting, construction work and cooking, have been remarkably successful. Despite a lack of even a high school education...hundreds of Amish entrepreneurs have built profitable businesses based on the Amish values of high quality, integrity and hard work. A 2004 Goshen College study reported that the failure rate of Amish businesses is less than 5 percent, compared with a national small-business default rate that is far higher.[1]

How do the Amish go into business without going against their values?

As one Amish man said, "If we hang on to our beards, buggies, and bonnets only so we can sell trinkets, we will indeed have sold our souls and our birthright for a bowl of porridge. Or to the other extreme, if we sacralize the name Amish to the point that we can hardly use it at all, we will have missed the point, which is that our lives are to be a light to the world and a service to Christ."[2]

With the shift into entrepreneurship, of course, comes other challenges to the Amish way of life, such as greater wealth, new technologies, less time spent at home with family, and even mothers working outside of the home. How the Amish will face these challenges as their world slowly changes remains to be seen.

FREE TIME, VACATIONS, AND ENTERTAINMENT

What do the Amish do for fun?

First of all, unlike average Americans who work hard now so they can play hard later, the Amish don't necessarily see work and play as mutually exclusive. Though they work incredibly hard, they almost always have time to enjoy conversation as they feed the animals, take a break from cooking to cuddle with the baby, or even set aside chores altogether for afternoon to go sledding in freshly fallen snow.

Once the workday is done, however, they do enjoy a number of leisure pursuits, such as:

- visiting friends and relatives
- playing sports such as volleyball, softball, and croquet
- enjoying card games and board games
- reading, writing letters, and relaxing
- hunting, fishing, and camping

Do they ever take vacations?

Yes, though these are usually inexpensive and may not involve traveling long distances. Families might go camping for several days or take an extended trip to visit relatives. While traveling, they might visit a museum or zoo or national park.

Do they play sports?

Yes, in moderation, though sports are frowned upon in some districts, at least for adults.

Do they watch sports?

They rarely attend live games, though many Amish will keep up with their favorite sports teams through the newspaper or via word of mouth.

Do they allow dancing?

No. They consider dancing to be worldly and immodest.

Do they play instruments?

While the Amish enjoy music, they do not usually play instruments. They like to sing and will often do so in church, school, and at home, without accompaniment.

Amish youth regularly have group singings, which also provide ample opportunities for flirting.

What are "singings"?

An important ritual of Amish youth, singings offer a time for teens to gather in a wholesome, supervised environment and sing hymns together.

The goal of singings is to socialize (and perhaps even find a mate). Held in various Amish homes, the events can last several hours and may include outdoor games. Snacks are usually served as well.

How the do the Amish celebrate special occasions?

For the Amish, fun almost always includes getting together with family and friends. Ask them how they celebrated the previous special occasion or holiday, and they will likely tell you who came over and what they had to eat.

Gatherings may also include board or card games such as Dutch Blitz or outdoor activities such as volleyball, archery, sledding, skating, swimming, or softball.

Do they celebrate birthdays?

Yes. Like the non-Amish, they will have birthday parties—even surprise parties—or dinner celebrations where they give cards and gifts and eat cake and ice cream.

Do they celebrate holidays, such as Christmas?

Yes, though perhaps not to nearly as much excess as many non-Amish do. Most Amish celebrate the basic holy days, such as Good Friday, Easter, Pentecost, and Christmas. (Some Amish groups also include the day after Easter and the day after Christmas in their celebration.) Religious holidays usually involve fasting and worship services and then food and fellowship.

At Christmastime, the children may put on a program at school, followed by a gift exchange with their friends. Decorations around the house, if any, are simple and homemade. On Christmas morning, families will share a time of prayer and devotions, and then modest gifts may be exchanged. Christmas dinner is enjoyed that day or the next and often includes friends and extended family members.

What about secular holidays, such as Halloween?

Though some Amish may exchange valentines or gather together for the occasional Labor Day picnic, they tend to ignore most secular holidays, especially those that relate to the military, such as Memorial Day and Veterans Day. They do not celebrate Halloween.

What community events do the Amish participate in for fun?

The Amish frequently enjoy social events that blend work and play, such as barn raisings, work frolics, and quilting bees.

They are also known for "mud sales" and other auctions, which provide ample opportunity for fun and fellowship.

What is a "work frolic"?

A common Amish practice, frolics are events that combine socializing with working toward common, practical goals. Frolics can be on a grand scale, such as with barn raisings, or on a far more modest scale, such as when several women get together for canning or quilting.

What is a "mud sale"?

PA Dutch Country, the official tourism bureau of Lancaster County, defines a mud sale as "an annual auction/sale at one of a number of local fire companies. The sales, appropriately named for the condition of the thawing ground, attract thousands of people looking for bargains on anything from Amish quilts and antiques to lumber, buggies and lawn equipment."[1]

PART THREE:
PASSAGES

He called me up and I kneeled, bowing my head, barely able to comprehend his words. Thankfully, I'd listened closely in class. When it was time, the water splashed over my kapp, over my forehead, rushing down my face. I tipped my head upward, smiling. When I stood and started back to my seat, brushing the wetness from my face, I caught Luke's eye. He nodded solemnly.

—Excerpted from *The Amish Bride*
by Mindy Starns Clark and Leslie Gould

22

CHILDHOOD, FAMILY, AND OLD AGE

What is a typical Amish childhood like?
Ideally, an Amish childhood is filled with God, love, work, fun, and family—often all at the same time. Unlike modern Americans, the Amish do not strongly delineate between worktime and playtime. Instead, they often combine the two, creating an industrious and satisfying lifestyle. With such large families and close-knit communities, someone always seems to be available to share the load, the learning, and the laughter.

Amish children also spend considerably more time interacting with the older members of their family. Often, several generations live under one roof, which gives plenty of access between children and their grandparents.

Are Amish children given chores?
Yes. From a very early age, Amish children are taught that working hard is a vitally important virtue, and they are expected to learn how to clean, plan and cook meals, guide a horse and buggy, plow a field, and more. On Amish farms, young children may be given a small animal—such as a chicken, duck, or goat—that they alone must care for, which instills a strong work ethic and a sense of responsibility.

What role do the parents play in this?
When Amish children are growing up, their parents invest an enormous amount of time teaching them, guiding them by example, and working with them. As one Amish father said about a farm chore, "I could do this a lot faster by myself, but how else is he going to learn?" Boys and girls may work alongside their fathers in the fields or the

workshop for hours each day. Girls are also often in the kitchen with their mothers, cooking or sewing or learning some other domestic skill.

Are they paid for these jobs? If not, is there some way for Amish youth to earn money?

If children want something, they are encouraged to work for it, as the Amish believe that a gift given too easily too soon robs children of the joy of earning it for themselves. Thus, most Amish families teach their children basic business principles, and older children may even derive a small income from their own produce stand or other home-based business.

Do parents spend much time discussing religion in the home?

Family devotions and prayer time are a mainstay, but outright religious instruction and theological introspection are rare for most Amish families. Instead, parents focus on quietly living out the principles of what they call *Demut* (the German word for humility) and expect their children to do the same. By the time the kids reach school age, they are usually well-behaved, respectful, unpretentious, unentitled, and secure in their place in the family and the community.

Do the children like this lifestyle?

An Amish childhood may not be as idyllic as it looks in pastel paintings and picture postcards, but in the best-case scenarios, it can be quite satisfying. Amish or not, it's hard to imagine children who wouldn't enjoy caring for their very own animals and living in a tight-knit community, surrounded by parents and siblings who love them and are willing to spend time with them.

What are the drawbacks to an Amish childhood?

In my opinion, the biggest problem for children on Amish farms is that they are often placed in unsafe situations, for example:

- Infants and toddlers may be tended by older siblings who are still too young and inexperienced themselves to be able to provide proper care.
- Children are sometimes in close proximity to dangerous farm equipment, often while barefoot.
- Boys as young as six or seven work with large animals such as cows and horses, often in dangerous ways.

A friend of mine describes with horror the time she stopped to buy firewood from an Amish home, and as the father stood and chatted with them, he sent his three-year-old son to retrieve the ax. Personally, I have witnessed an Amish child of perhaps eight or nine single-handedly managing a team of six horses while perched, barefoot, on the narrow standing platform of a huge piece of farming machinery. (To see a photograph I took of this, visit www.amishfaqs.com/helpful.php.)

Perhaps the average American tends to carry child safety a little too far in the opposite direction, but the Amish attitude on this topic can be disconcerting to the non-Amish, to say the least.

What roles do husbands and wives take in the family?

Amish husbands and wives generally assume traditional male-female roles in the family. The husband is typically the breadwinner, and the wife cares for the home and the children.

Mothers generally do not work outside of the home unless absolutely necessary. They will, however, participate in a family business by keeping the books or staffing roadside stands. They may also have a small side business, such as quilt making.

What happens to the elderly? Do the Amish use nursing homes?

The Amish do not generally use nursing homes or retirement homes for their elderly. Instead, the elderly will live with their children and/or grandchildren, often in an expanded section of the house.

For example, when a couple's children are grown, they might pass down the farm to one of the younger generation and move themselves into what is known as a *Grossdaadi Haus,* a smaller structure connected to or nearby the main house, much like an "in-law suite." There, the elder parents live out the rest of their lives, helping with the younger ones when they can, providing wisdom and companionship to the family, and growing old with dignity and grace.

23

SCHOOL

Do Amish children go to public school?

Approximately 10 percent of all Amish children go to public schools. The remaining 90 percent attend private parochial schools run by their communities. The Amish call their students "scholars."

What does an Amish schoolhouse look like?

Amish schoolhouses usually consist of one or two rooms and are large enough to accommodate 25 to 30 children of various grade levels, with separate boys' and girls' outhouse-style bathrooms outside.

Do the Amish use school buses?

The children usually walk to school, but where distance is an issue, neighboring parents may take turns or school buses are hired.

How many teachers are in each school, and what are their qualifications?

Each school has one teacher, usually an unmarried Amish woman in her late teens or early twenties who has been chosen because of her Christian character, Amish values, and teaching ability. Two-room schoolhouses or single-room schoolhouses with more than 30 children may have a second teacher or a teacher's assistant. Older students often help with the younger students.

How about kids with special needs?

In schools for Amish children with special needs, the teacher-student ratio is about one to four.

At what age do Amish children first enter school?

Just as their non-Amish counterparts do, Amish children enter first grade around age six.

What sort of schedule do Amish schools follow?

School hours and term lengths are similar to those in non-Amish schools, though the Amish generally don't take as much time off for holidays. In Lancaster County, for example, Christmas is only a two-day break, which means the school year ends in early May.

Is it true that they only go to school until the eighth grade?

Yes. Amish children conclude their formal education with the eighth grade.

Have the Amish always had their own schools?

No. Prior to the late 1930s, the Amish usually attended small, rural public schools in or near their communities. From 1937 to 1954, as public school boards began consolidating these into larger schools, the Amish became concerned that their children were being taught too far from home by teachers the family didn't know, they were getting an education that neither complemented nor facilitated an agricultural lifestyle, and they were being exposed to too much of the outside world. Afraid that their communities were being undermined, some Amish responded by building their own private schools, hiring their own teachers, and limiting education to the eighth grade.

Was that legal?

Initially, school officials considered the Amish teachers uncertified and undereducated and their lack of high school–level instruction unacceptable. A period of unrest and controversy followed, and some Amish fathers were arrested, fined, and even jailed for taking a stand. Some compromises were reached, but the issue finally came to a head in 1972, when the case of *Wisconsin v. Yoder* reached the U.S. Supreme Court. Finding in favor of the Amish, the court determined once and for all that Amish schools were to be allowed and that forcing Amish children to attend any school past the eighth grade was a violation of their religious freedom.

Who oversees Amish schools? Is there such a thing as an Amish Board of Education?

Amish schools are directed by small boards of local Amish fathers who approve the curriculum, hire the teachers, maintain the buildings, and oversee the budgets.

What subjects are taught in school?

Though the curriculum varies from district to district, most Amish students study arithmetic, spelling, reading, grammar, history, geography, social studies, German, and penmanship.

What about science?

Amish farmers deal frequently with the science of agriculture, but science as a school subject is considered suspect. Thus, except for nature studies, science is generally not included in the curriculum.

How about religion?

Religion is not taught in school, though Amish values are woven throughout their textbooks. Some religious rituals are included in the school day, such as the reading of an opening prayer.

Are any subjects prohibited?

Beyond religion and science, classes are also not likely to be given in computers, music, art, drama, or physical education.

What language do they use in school?

Classes are taught in English, and the children are expected to speak English both in the classroom and on the playground. Most first graders start school with only a rudimentary knowledge of English, so they are usually given some leeway until they become fluent.

What does an Amish person do if he or she wants to learn more after eighth grade?

Amish adults who require further learning on a particular topic, such as bookkeeping, will teach themselves, learn from a coworker, or take a correspondence course. In some communities, when a high school diploma is required for a job, Amish youth may be allowed to get a general equivalency diploma (GED).

It sounds as though Amish schools have a different focus than non-Amish ones. What are their goals with education?

Amish schools do not normally emphasize critical analysis, independent thinking, creativity, or individuality. Instead, they focus on the Amish values of obedience, respect, kindness, cooperation, and submission. Such a limited education may not prepare the Amish to function in a high-tech world, but it does sufficiently prepare them for Amish life and work.

What is the parent's role in an Amish child's education?

The National PTA has published a list of the "Top 10 Things Teachers Wish Parents Would Do." Not surprisingly, Amish parents have already been doing many of these things for years, such as setting a good example and encouraging students to do their best. In fact, number ten is central to the way Amish parents operate: "'Accept your responsibility as parents.' Don't expect the school and teachers to take over your obligations as parents. Teach children self-discipline and respect for others at home—don't rely on teachers and schools to teach these basic behaviors and attitudes." [1]

The Amish would never dream of leaving parental matters such as those described above in the hands of teachers. Instead, they know they are the primary authority figures in their children's lives and are responsible to raise them up in the way that they should go.

RUMSPRINGA

What makes someone "Amish"? Are they simply born into it?

No. Despite the common use of the term "Amish child" (even in this book), there is no such thing. The more correct wording would be "child of Amish parents" or "child in an Amish community." That's because people aren't *born* Amish; they must *become* Amish, which is a voluntary process that happens at the cusp of adulthood, usually in the late teens or early twenties. That's when those who have been raised in Amish homes decide whether they are going to accept the Amish faith and be baptized into its membership. Only if they do will they actually be considered Amish.

Is it true that Amish teenagers are encouraged to move out and go wild?

No. Among the non-Amish, a lot of misconceptions exist about the period in Amish youth known as *Rumspringa*. A Pennsylvania Dutch term that means "running around," *Rumspringa* does not involve moving out of the home, nor does it typically include excessive partying or other wild behavior. Instead, the goal of *Rumspringa* is simply to relax the rules a bit to allow teenagers to experience a taste of the outside world, to find a mate (parents hope), and to give teens enough freedom to make an informed, independent, and mature decision about whether they want to become Amish or leave the faith community and forge a new life on their own outside of the church.

If they don't choose to join the church, are they shunned?

No. Those who have been raised in Amish homes but opt not to join the Amish faith themselves are able to maintain relationships with their Amish family and friends.

What age do they go on *Rumspringa* and what is it like?

Rumspringa usually begins around age 16 and lasts for several years. During this time, though teens still live at home and have all of the same obligations and responsibilities as before, the rules of the *Ordnung* are relaxed. Parents and church leaders "look the other way" as teens are allowed to experiment with their newfound freedom. Teens get their own private bedroom and sometimes even slip away at night to meet up with friends or dates.

Is *Rumspringa* the same everywhere?

No. In a conservative district, *Rumspringa* might include, at most, flirting at a group singing or riding home from church with someone of the opposite sex in a courting wagon. In a more liberal district, *Rumspringa* can mean obtaining a driver's license, buying a car, using electronics, and having a cell phone, among other things

Do Amish teens ever take their freedom too far?

It happens. In worst-case scenarios, teens may get involved with sex, drugs, alcohol, smoking, or spending their weekends at rowdy *Rumspringa* parties, notorious beer bashes that include both Amish and non-Amish teenagers and young adults.

When does *Rumspringa* come to an end?

Young adults in Amish communities must eventually choose between turning their backs on the world and accepting the faith of their parents, or making somewhat of a break from their homes and family and fully embracing the outside world. All teens know that if they decide to go with the church, they are making a lifelong commitment. As a part of the baptism process, they will take vows that commit them to the community, the church leadership, and the *Ordnung* until the day they die.

Do many of them make that choice?

Yes. Eighty-five percent of teens raised in Amish homes choose to join the church.

What is "bundling"?

In some conservative districts, teens on *Rumspringa* may be allowed to enjoy an old Amish custom known as *Uneheliche beischlaf*, the practice of "bundling" or "bed courtship." Bundling allows an unmarried male and female to spend the night together in the same bed, ostensibly without having sex. They may each be wrapped in their own blanket, or she may wear a special preventative gown. The couple is left alone in the female's bedroom, and the parents go on to bed. The young man is allowed to spend most of the night but is expected to leave the home before morning milking time, which is usually around four or four thirty.

Is bundling a common practice?

No. According to author Richard Stevick in his book *Growing Up Amish: The Teenage Years*, bundling was brought to America by European immigrants in the eighteenth century and was far more prevalent in the past than it is today. He estimates that fewer than 10 percent of Amish districts still allow bundling. Most Amish seem reticent to discuss the custom at all.

Why would bundling be allowed? Wouldn't it lead to premarital sex?

Premarital sex is not a permitted aspect of the bundling experience, though most critics of the practice insist it often becomes inevitable. In the event that a premarital pregnancy results, most Amish teens will quickly join the church and then get married. Some critics charge that this is the whole point—to force the couple into church membership and marriage because of an unintended pregnancy.

Proponents of bundling assert that it teaches self-discipline while allowing the couple to get to know each other in a private setting.

25

BAPTISM

Where do the Amish learn about their beliefs? Do they have Sunday school, Training Union, or something similar?

The only formal religious instruction that most Amish ever receive are the classes that prepare them for baptism. These special classes are held every other Sunday for eight or nine sessions total and are taught by the bishop and the ministers. Students who complete all sessions in a satisfactory manner are then eligible for membership in the Amish church.

What is the process for getting baptized?

When a young person decides he wants to be baptized, he presents himself for the first of eight or nine classes that will be taught over the course of several months. Baptisms occur only once a year, so many parents of teens hold their breath, waiting to see if their children are among those who choose to attend the class. If not, their children will have another year of *Rumspringa* before their next opportunity arises to do so.

How important is it to Amish parents that their children join the church?

It's very important. In fact, many Amish consider themselves successful parents only if their children join the church.

At what age are the Amish baptized?

Most candidates for baptism are in their late teens or early twenties.

What do they learn in the baptism classes?

The classes primarily focus on the Dordrecht Confession of Faith, a document written in 1632 that espouses the key beliefs of Anabaptism. Candidates learn in depth about each of the document's 18 articles and in many cases will also be taught the specifics of their own local *Ordnung*. During the months that candidates are attending these every-other-Sunday classes, they are expected to eliminate all trappings of *Rumspringa* from their lives, which means selling their cars, getting rid of their English clothes, giving up technological devices, growing out their hair, and so on. In some districts, they must quit attending secular weekend parties by the third session in order to move into full compliance with the *Ordnung*.

Are they under a lot of pressure to follow through and get baptized?

Yes and no. Certainly, family and community members may exert significant pressure and expectation. On the other hand, throughout the preparation process the attendees are asked repeatedly if they are sure that this is what they want. In fact, each session begins with the youth stating, "I am a seeker desiring to be part of this church of God." The Amish strongly emphasize informed, voluntary adult baptism. So in a sense there is pressure in both directions.

What happens to those who decide not to go through with the classes or baptism?

Candidates who are hesitant, rebellious, or too questioning may decide they were not ready after all and drop out of the classes—perhaps just until the next year, when they will be more certain of their decision.

What if they know for certain they're done for good, that they will not be joining the Amish church now or in the future? What happens to them?

They are not shunned, but neither are they treated as adults in the Amish community. Essentially, they live in a sort of in-between world, where their ultimate choice is either to leave for good or to stay and become baptized.

How about the ones who decide to go through with the course of classes? What happens for them?

Those who make it to the end have one final session (which includes their parents), the day before baptism Sunday, where once again they are asked if they are certain they want to proceed. At this point, the male candidates are also asked if they are willing to serve in the ministry if they are ever chosen by lot.

What happens on the day of the baptism?

Baptism is usually held on the same Sunday as the fall communion service. Candidates take vows and then kneel in front of the bishop, who confirms their vows and baptizes them one by one. Amish baptism is done by the bishop placing his cupped hands on each head as the deacon pours water into those hands from a pitcher. After all are baptized, the bishop welcomes each male in turn with a holy kiss while his wife does the same to the females.

Once baptized, members are bound to the Amish faith for the rest of their lives.

What if they later change their mind? Can they leave the church?

Those who chose to leave the church after baptism are usually excommunicated and shunned. See chapter 10, "Shunning," for more information.

26

COURTSHIP AND MARRIAGE

How do engagements work in the Amish community?

For an engagement to be made official, the groom must go to his bishop, declare his intentions, and acquire a *Zeugnis*, which is a letter of good standing from his church. If the bishop is aware of any sinful behavior or need for correction, he deals with it at that time.

Once the groom acquires the *Zeugnis*, he delivers it to the bride's minister or deacon. That church leader will visit the bride, confirm she desires to marry the groom, and discuss any sin or other concerns in her life. After this meeting, if all is satisfactory, the leader will wait until the appropriate time and then "publish" or announce the engagement to the church.

Is it true that the Amish are extremely secretive about their dating lives?

Somewhat. Courtship among the Amish is done with discretion, and engagements are not usually made public until one to six weeks before the wedding. Prior to that, a bride and groom's closest friends and family members may be told, but otherwise only the church leaders are informed and not the congregation at large.

When do the Amish get married?

In some settlements, weddings are limited to certain times of the year and even specific days of the week. Lancaster County weddings, for example, are held on Tuesdays and Thursdays in October, November, and December. Weddings in Geauga County, Ohio, are held in the summer.

Can an Amish person marry outside of the faith?

Not if they intend to remain in the Amish church, as rules require both bride and groom to have been baptized within the Amish faith.

What is an Amish wedding like?

Amish weddings can be quite large, often with 300 to 500 guests. The Amish don't use caterers, so the food preparation alone can be a tremendous undertaking. Fortunately, plenty of volunteers are always available to help out, and the communities have been through so many weddings before that everyone is familiar with the various duties required.

Weddings are usually held in the bride's parents' home, barn, or shop. The regular Sunday benches are used, though if the wedding is large, benches from other nearby communities may be needed as well. In a carefully orchestrated event, family and friends work to prepare the wedding feast and ready the home for the celebration.

How about the wedding ceremony itself?

Amish wedding ceremonies are similar in many ways to their regular Sunday worship services. As the congregation sings the opening hymns, the couple is brought into a separate room with the bishop and ministers for a time of "admonition and encouragement" called the *Abroth*. This lasts about 20 or 30 minutes, and then all rejoin the congregation for the rest of the service. As on Sundays, an opening sermon, a prayer, a Bible reading, and a main sermon are included. The bride and groom each have two attendants.

How long is the wedding ceremony?

About three hours.

What do the bride and groom wear?

In most districts, the couple wear brand-new versions of their usual Sunday attire, with one exception: The groom sports his first "real" Amish hat, one with a broader brim to indicate he is married.

Once the ceremony is over, the bride will switch from the black head covering of a single girl to the white *kapp* of a married woman.

Do they exchange wedding rings?

No.

Do they take vows?

During the main sermon, the bishop asks the couple a series of questions, the affirmation of which will serve as their vows. This is followed by the reading of a prayer and the pronouncing of the couple as man and wife.

Does the groom "kiss the bride"?

No. The Amish rarely indulge in public displays of affection, even between married couples. Thus, the bride and groom do not kiss but instead return to their seats for the rest of the service. Additional sermons and commentary are given by other church leaders, followed by final prayers and songs.

Is there a reception after the wedding?

Yes. The type of post-wedding celebration varies from district to district but always focuses on the newly married couple and includes a feast. Eating may also be done in shifts as various volunteers serve.

The celebration may also include other festivities, such as:

- the opening of gifts
- an afternoon singing
- pranks played on the bride and groom, such as hiding their washing machine or dismantling their bed
- a game of walk-a-mile among the *Youngie* (young people)
- pairing off of the unmarried young people for an evening of dining and fellowship
- a wedding supper
- cake and ice cream

In some settlements, the celebration can continue late into the night.

Does the couple go on a honeymoon?

Sometimes, though honeymoon travel is not common. Typically, the new husband and wife will spend their wedding night at the home of the bride's parents. The very next morning, they are expected to rise with everyone else at four or five to pitch in with the massive cleanup effort. Other close friends or relatives may join in to help as well.

It is not unusual for the bride and groom to continue living in his or her parents' home for several weeks or months following the wedding. For some, this period of time may be considered their "honeymoon." On the weekends, the couple pays visits to the numerous relatives and friends who came to their wedding. In each home, they will be greeted warmly, share a meal, enjoy conversation, and in many cases be given their wedding presents.

When the visits have all been made, the couple might move into a small home of their own, preferably one located near other family members. They will set up housekeeping there and finally begin their life together in their own home as husband and wife.

What is the connection between celery and Amish weddings?

In some regions, despite all of the secrecy regarding courtships, nosy community members can usually figure out which families will be having a fall wedding by the amount of celery they planted in their garden that year. Celery is a late-growing vegetable, so it's a common fixture at weddings both as a main food and in table decorations. If the guest list will be large, as it usually is, the celery must be grown in great quantities, far more than a family would otherwise need.

Do the Amish allow divorce?

No. The church does not sanction divorce, though separation is not unheard of.

27

DEATH

Do the Amish have funeral homes? If not, who handles the details when someone dies?

There are no Amish funeral homes. When an Amish person dies, volunteers from the community step in and handle funeral preparations, housework, and farmwork. This leaves the family free to focus on the relatives and friends who come to pay their respects.

For the Amish, funerals are very uniform by design. Tradition dictates everything from casket style to burial clothing to the post-funeral meal.

Medically, is there anything different in the way Amish deaths are handled?

The Amish prefer to die at home whenever possible. Whether death comes there or in a hospital, the body of the deceased is handled in the same manner: A non-Amish mortician retrieves it and embalms it.

After that, the body is returned to the home. There, family members of the same sex dress the embalmed body in burial clothes and place the deceased in a simple wooden casket. Cosmetics are not used when preparing the body.

Do the Amish have wakes or visitations and if so, where are they held?

Yes, the Amish have visitations for family and friends, usually in the home of the deceased. Once the body has been prepared, it goes on display in the casket in a main room of the first floor, where it will remain until the funeral.

What is an Amish funeral like?

Funerals are usually held on the third day after death, unless that happens to fall on a Sunday. Services take place in the home and are about an hour and a half long, consisting of various ministers giving sermons and reading hymns, Scriptures, and prayers. There are no songs, eulogies, or flowers.

After the funeral, everyone proceeds to an Amish cemetery where a grave has been dug by hand by family or friends. A brief word is offered graveside, and then the casket, which typically has no handles, is lowered into the ground with ropes and covered with dirt.

Following the ceremony, close family and friends return to the home where they share a meal that has been prepared by the community.

How are friends and relatives notified when an Amish person dies?

When an Amish person dies, news spreads throughout the community by word of mouth. Distant relatives and friends may have to be contacted more directly.

Where do the Amish bury their dead?

In Amish cemeteries, which are very simple and uniform. In a final display of humility, the headstones are almost always of equal size and contain no extra information or fancy embellishments.

Part Four:
OUTSIDE WORLD

The matching clothes, immaculate farms, and whitewashed houses and barns had a stylized appearance. I liked things uniform. It appealed to my sterile sense of decor. But none of this was sterile. It was all very much alive. The people. The scents wafting through my open window. The vibrant colors snapping on the lines. It was orderly and patterned and obviously it all had a purpose.

—Excerpted from *The Amish Midwife*
by Mindy Starns Clark and Leslie Gould

US AND THEM

Are outsiders allowed to join the Amish church, or do you have to be born into it?

The Amish allow converts to their faith, though successful, permanent conversions of outsiders into the Amish church are rare.

What obstacles would a potential convert face?

For starters, they would need to learn Pennsylvania Dutch, which is the language of the Amish home and community. Beyond that, they would have to deal with the lack of technology (no computers, telephones, electricity, etc.), the need for frugality, and more than likely the hard work of farming. Essentially, they would have to change their ways of doing almost everything from heating a home to educating children to cooking dinner.

These would all be incredibly difficult adjustments, especially for one who has grown up in a world of relative luxury and modern conveniences.

How does the Amish mentality differ from the modern American mind-set?

From a very young age, the Amish are taught that one must continually die to self, resist pride at all costs, and often place the greater good of others over personal desires. Their goal is to live in constant obedience and submission—to God, to church leaders, and to one another. For the average person living in a postmodern world, the thought of sacrificing personal identity for the greater good of the community is foreign indeed. Encouraged from a young age to stand out from the crowd and be proud of our accomplishments, the non-Amish learn to celebrate individuality, creativity, and personal freedom. Eschewing these things for the Amish frame of mind would be difficult, if not nearly impossible, for anyone who was not raised in that culture.

How can I meet an Amish person face-to-face?

Several ways might be to visit an Amish area and patronize Amish businesses, stay in an Amish bed-and-breakfast, or have dinner in an Amish home that regularly hosts visitors.

To do any of the above, you might start with a simple Google search for such phrases as "dine in an Amish home" or "spend the night on an Amish farm." If that doesn't work, try contacting the tourist information center in the area you'll be visiting, as they will often be able to point you in the right direction.

Why do the Amish call the non-Amish "English" or "Englishers"?

Because we speak English as our primary language instead of the German dialect they use.

TOURISM AND THE MEDIA

What is the draw for Amish tourism?
In their book *The Amish and the Media*, authors Diane Zimmerman Umble and David Weaver-Zercher address our collective obsession with all things Amish. They state that for those who operate from different assumptions about dress, travel, education, technology, and success, the religiously informed decisions that the Amish have made over the past 150 years have produced not only a visibly distinct culture but also a viscerally fascinating one.

What is it that is so appealing about the Amish way of life?
Tourists often come to Amish settlements to participate in what Umble and Weaver-Zercher call "the myth of the pastoral." This myth implies that Amish life is wholesome, old fashioned, simple, perfect, and good; dining on a bounty of farm-fresh delights every day, the Amish have no cares or problems, are free from all technology, and are in fact uniquely pure and special.

No wonder we come to gawk. The Amish-based tourism industry tends to focus on the more iconic, picturesque parts of their culture: their charming manner of dress and speech, their patchwork farms, their homemade food, and their beautiful quilts and furniture.

Is this unrealistic?
Of course. The Amish are human beings with normal human problems, conflicts, and frustrations. Their history has its unattractive parts, as does their society. Much about the Amish people is good, but they are not, in fact, perfect. They are simply people.

Does tourism exploit the Amish?

In many cases, yes. The word "Amish" draws tourists and custom-
ers, which results in the good, the bad, and the ugly. For example, in
Lancaster County, Pennsylvania, it feels as though for every helpful
information center there's a neon-signed tourist trap; for every taste-
ful furniture store offering Amish-made goods, there's a cartoon ren-
dering of a bearded men in a black hat advertising "authentic" Amish
fast food.

Why is that bad?

Because these are blatant attempts to milk the Amish cash cow by
those who have no claim to the moniker. From "Amish goods" that
were actually made in China to "Amish buggy rides" given by non-
Amish wearing costumes to tacky tourist shops overflowing with
horse and buggy pencil sharpeners, these are all "Amish" things that
no real Amish person would have any use for.

Where did our obsession with all things Amish come from?

According to Umble and Weaver-Zercher, this fascination "is not
an inevitable, let alone accidental, result of differences between the
Amish and the English. Rather, this fascination has been created and
sustained to a large degree by the media."[1] No doubt, our ideas of the
Amish people, what they believe, and how they live are greatly influenced by the tourism, film, television, publishing, and news industries.

When was Amish life first depicted in popular culture?

In 1985, the Peter Weir movie *Witness* became a worldwide hit. Set in
the midst of Amish country, the movie, which starred Harrison Ford
and Kelly McGillis, earned two Oscars and almost $70 million at the
box office. To this day, many people's knowledge about the Amish is
limited to this single film.

Does *Witness* accurately depict the Amish?

Witness has been criticized by many Amish as being inconsistent
with their lifestyle and culture. This shouldn't be too surprising. The
purpose of a romantic drama, after all, is to entertain, not inform.

Filmmakers have always taken liberties with the truth in order to create more exciting stories. Unfortunately, a person whose entire knowledge of the Amish comes from feature films like *Witness*—not to mention *For Richer or Poorer, Kingpin,* and others—is at best underinformed and at worst sorely misinformed.

What about documentaries? Do they give us a more realistic perspective?

Documentaries often fall at two ends of the spectrum, what Umble and Weaver-Zercher call either "sympathetic, myth-enhancing pastorals like *A People of Preservation* or myth-busting and highly entertaining but narrowly focused and nonrepresentative sensationalism like *Devil's Playground*."[2] Neither of these two films plays fast and loose with the facts, but both provide specific angles on certain facets of Amish life. This, in turn, causes many people to apply those narrow truths to the Amish as a whole, which is a mistake.

If feature films and the documentaries aren't getting it right, how about reality TV?

In July 2004, the reality show *Amish in the City* debuted, featuring five Amish youth on *Rumspringa* in a modern home where they lived for a time among five non-Amish youth. By filming the inevitable culture clash, the producers hoped to highlight the similarities and differences between two such disparate worlds. In the end, the series was criticized as exploitative and offensive. It also didn't do much to advance the cause of truth about Amish life.

Now with the latest offerings in this genre—the reality shows *Breaking Amish* and *Amish Mafia*—things seem to have gone from bad to worse.

Are the Amish accurately represented by mainstream news media?

The news media cannot always be counted on for accuracy or balance when it comes to the Amish either. News reports still need a hook, after all, and the hooks that come from an Amish drug bust or a travesty of violence have less to do with the incidents themselves than with our image of who the Amish are and how the incidents relate to that.

How did media respond to the Amish school shooting at Nickel Mines in 2006?

One need look no further than the media coverage of this incident to see how shockingly fast the big story turned from the violence perpetrated on a group of schoolchildren to the "larger issues" of Amish forgiveness. I would contend that the news media did both the Amish and the non-Amish a great disservice by focusing their reports on the forgiveness angle rather than on larger, more important issues, such as school violence, child safety, and mental illness.

If movies and TV are getting it wrong, where can I go to find truthful, helpful information about the Amish?

By drawing information from the following sources, one can leave fallacies and agendas behind and instead focus on the fascinating, complex, and *true* world of the Amish.

Academia. Thanks to esteemed authors and scholars such as Donald Kraybill, David Weaver-Zercher, John Hostetler, Richard Stevick, and Steven Nolt, numerous resources are available for those who want to get an accurate, balanced view of the Amish.

Fiction. Certainly, Amish fiction authors bring to any story their own slant and agenda, but most authors of Amish fiction seem to be taking pains to get their facts correct and present them in a balanced manner. By setting fictional tales in realistic worlds, Amish fiction authors are inviting readers to a fuller understanding of Amish life in all its shades of black, white, and gray.

Historical societies and information centers. Many historical organizations offer accurate and interesting information about the Amish and other Anabaptist groups. In some regions, these places offer helpful volunteers, printed resources, and even tour guide services. Should you choose to visit a region of Amish tourism, you would do well to begin your visit not with a flashy simulated "Amish experience" but with the local historical society or tourist information center. See the Resources section near the end of this book for more information.

How did Amish fiction first come about?

In 1997, a literary genre was born with the release of *The Shunning*, author Beverly Lewis's fictional tale of Amish life based on her own grandmother's experiences. As more books from Lewis and other authors followed, readers were able to get an inside peek into Amish life, and the genre's popularity has continued to grow.

Why is Amish fiction so popular?

According to Associated Press reporter Eric Gorski, these books are a hit with those "attracted by a simpler time, curiosity about cloistered communities and admiration for the strong, traditional faith of the Amish."[3]

As a writer of Amish fiction myself, I know that part of the allure is the ability to explore a world so foreign to us and yet for some reason so appealing. Through the lives of characters on a page, we can all become Amish for a while, even if only in our imaginations.

Some fiction authors depict the Amish in a positive light, while others present a somewhat negative view. Which is more accurate?

The Amish experience can vary between various settlements and districts. As far as I can tell, both angles have some basis in fact. The Amish are human, after all, and while they have their share of problems, there is also much to admire about their values and lifestyle.

As an author, I try to present a balanced picture of the Amish in my fiction, neither idealizing nor demonizing them but instead creating characters and situations that are realistic and compelling.

How do the Amish feel about Amish fiction?

They find our interest in them baffling, but many of them read these books themselves. In my experience, they enjoy those authors who present the Amish faith in a balanced, positive light but often take umbrage with those who do not. As an Amish woman once commented about a work of fiction she had read, "It was upsetting, to say the least. The bishop in that book was a monster, but my bishop is the dearest, kindest man I have ever known."

TRAGEDY AND FORGIVENESS

The Amish are known for their forgiveness. Why is this so?

Because they take very seriously the biblical admonition "Do not judge, or you too will be judged" (Matthew 7:1). They forgive others so that God will forgive them of their sins.

But what about extreme situations when forgiveness seems impossible?

Their goal is still complete forgiveness, no matter what. Certainly, in horrific situations such as the Amish school shootings at Nickel Mines in 2006, this takes a nearly heroic effort to accomplish. But as one Amish man told me, forgiveness in a case like this isn't necessarily a onetime thing but is instead an ongoing pursuit, a matter of original forgiveness and then *re*-forgiveness, as needed.

What happened with the shooting at Nickel Mines?

One of the most tragic events in Amish history was the shooting of innocent children on October 2, 2006, in the town of Nickel Mines, Pennsylvania. On that otherwise quiet Monday morning, a local non-Amish man entered a one-room Amish schoolhouse, surprising the students and teachers and taking them hostage at gunpoint. He forced the adults and boys out of the building and then barricaded himself inside with the girls, whom he lined up along the chalkboard and bound at the ankles with wire and plastic ties.

Though police responded promptly to the event, they were unable to stop the gunman from opening fire on the girls and then himself. In the end, the incident left five Amish girls dead and five more in critical condition. Also dead, by suicide, was the gunman himself, whose motives have never been fully understood. Experts think he may have been struggling with mental illness. He was a resident of the area and reportedly had no grudges or ill will against the Amish.

Did the Amish community really forgive him? How could they do that?

The Amish, though heartbroken, astounded the world by responding to the event by offering nearly immediate forgiveness for the gunman and comfort for his surviving family members. Beginning just hours after the shooting, members of the Amish community started visiting the family, about 30 Amish attended his funeral, and Amish church leaders even set up a charitable trust for his widow and children.

How did the world respond?

Surprisingly, such rapid and complete forgiveness in word and deed drew harsh criticism from many directions. Opinions were expressed in public forums by writers who, lacking full knowledge of Amish culture or firsthand familiarity with the event and its aftermath, blasted the Amish community's act of grace, often putting it in the wrong context. One *Boston Globe* columnist wrote, "Hatred is not always wrong, and forgiveness is not always deserved…I would not want to be like [the Amish], reacting to terrible crimes with dispassion and absolution."[1]

Had the reporter been there himself, he would have seen absolutely nothing dispassionate about the Amish response to the Nickel Mines tragedy. The sadness of the Amish was searing and deep. Their grief was overwhelmingly painful. Even now, years after the event, their heartache over the situation is sometimes palpable. Amish experts say that the act of forgiving the killer was not a dispassionate act, as the columnist claimed, but instead "a habit that's embedded in a way of life anchored in a 400-year history" and "the first step toward mending a social fabric that was rent by the schoolhouse shooting."[2] These far more accurate descriptions were provided by preeminent Amish scholars Donald B. Kraybill, Steven M. Nolt, and David L. Weaver-Zercher in *Amish Grace: How Forgiveness Transcended Tragedy.* That book sums up the "forgiveness controversy" with these words:

In a world where faith often justifies and magnifies revenge, and in a nation where some Christians use Scripture to fuel retaliation, the Amish response was indeed a surprise. Regardless of the details of the Nickel Mines story, one message rings clear: Religion was not used to justify rage and revenge but to inspire goodness, forgiveness, and grace. And that is the big lesson for the rest of us regardless of our faith or nationality.[3]

For the Amish families involved, how are they doing now? Have they fully recovered from the incident?

I recently dined in the home of one of the families whose lives were directly impacted by the shooting. Though the tragedy itself was not mentioned, I couldn't help but notice the sadness that still lingers in the mother's eyes, the heavy feeling of loss that permeates the entire family.

Certainly, they have continued on in the world of the living. Their gleaming floors, healthy animals, and overflowing gardens attest to that. For the most part, family life seems back to business as usual, their youngest child laughing at the dogs' antics, their teenager flashing a shy smile at his girlfriend.

But despite the years that have passed, the family is obviously still learning to adapt to what psychologists call a "new normal," one where children can be victims of a senseless crime but life goes on anyway. For this family, and indeed for all the Amish families touched by the tragedy, forgiveness is something they did in the beginning, yes, but as someone close to them once told me, it is also "something they must do over and over, sometimes each new day."

Is it true they don't like to talk about it?

Yes. Among the Amish, the tragedy at Nickel Mines has come to be known as "The Happening." They don't discuss it much anymore, at least not with outsiders. The schoolhouse has long since been torn down, its replacement built in a different style at a different location.

No longer the Nickel Mines School, it has been christened New Hope, a name that resonates with optimism for the future despite the past.

Of the five victims who survived the shooting, one lives with lingering medical issues, they have all had numerous surgeries, and one suffered extensive brain damage and is confined to a wheelchair. All five are currently living at home with their families, going on with their lives. My best impression of how the incident has impacted the Amish community at large came from a conversation with another Amish woman, one who wasn't directly connected to the victims or their families but grieved nonetheless. She and I weren't even talking about the shooting but about the *Ordnung* and infractions of rules and differences between districts. According to her, Nickel Mines put everything into perspective.

"We used to bicker more, have disagreements about this little rule and that little rule and who did what differently in which districts. Then something…bigger happened, something terrible," she said, her voice faltering for a moment, "and we realized all the arguing was so pointless. There were far more important matters in life."

Though I am not Amish, I knew exactly what she meant. Sometimes it takes a tragedy to put everything else into perspective.

31

WHY ARE THEY AMISH?

In the course of writing this book, I have thought a lot about Amish life. About the good and the bad, the pros and the cons.

Picturing myself in their world, I first think about the cons. I imagine all their rules and how I would chafe so strongly against them. I think of not being allowed to have electricity or choose my own style of clothing or pursue my education. I think of how I would resent being discouraged from having theological discussions or prohibited from singing along with a praise band in church. I look at my children and can't fathom limiting their education or their occupational choices. As charming as the Amish life can seem from the outside looking in, there are many reasons I would never want to be Amish.

And yet...

And yet there is much to be said for the Amish way of life, much to admire, much to emulate. Their peaceful existence. Their strong work ethic. The way they constantly strive for Christlikeness. It draws me in a way I don't quite understand. Still, I know that living in their world couldn't work for me.

What I've been trying to understand is why it works for *them*.

Truly, why are they Amish? As I researched this book, I came up with several answers to that question.

First, I believe the Amish find tremendous personal satisfaction in belonging to something bigger than themselves. Their incredibly strong family and community ties make the difficult parts of life easier, the rules worth following, the lifestyle worth living. Belonging to a group of believers with whom one worships, fellowships, goes to school, works, and plays would be incredibly fulfilling. Imagine knowing that if your barn burned down, your friends would show up and build you another one. Imagine facing catastrophic medical issues with the knowledge that your community would shoulder the financial burden beyond what you were able to pay. Imagine living in a community that was a real community, where everyone's duty was to love one another, care for one another, befriend one another, and even discipline one another—all because God requires them to. Imagine the safety net that would provide. In a world where we hardly know our next-door neighbors, the thought of being that strongly connected to an entire people group is appealing indeed.

Second, the family structure provides much to admire as well. The children of the Amish spend an enormous amount of time in the company of their parents. The Amish see childrearing as their most important job, and they are always instructing, loving, guiding, and teaching. Who wouldn't enjoy knowing that their highest calling was simply to be God in the flesh to one's own children?

Third, the Amish have a wonderful way to grow old. They have no institutions to care for the elderly. Instead, families stay together, with the older parents shifting into the *Grossdaadi Haus*, where they can age with grace and dignity. They often end their days right there at home.

Fourth is their calm and simple day-to-day life. Without televisions, things are quieter and more peaceful; without telephones and computers, life has far fewer interruptions. Given the Amish emphasis on simplicity and serenity, one can easily imagine lingering after dinner with the family, reading or sewing, sharing news of the day, the children quietly playing nearby.

Finally, I believe that the Amish enjoy living as they do because God is so very central to all of it. The Amish strive mightily to live within His will, follow the Scriptures, and truly be in the world but not of the world. For those who embrace Christ as Savior, theirs is a joyous and noble path indeed.

That's why it works for them.

Perhaps this is also why Amish fiction is so popular: Though we can't imagine life without modern conveniences and unlimited entertainment options, something is incredibly appealing to us about living fully for God in a home that is technology-free, family focused, and surrounded by a loving and supportive community. Through reading, we can experience all of that vicariously as we briefly visit their world.

But as we put away the books and come back out again, let us bring with us all that is fine and good and true about the Amish.

Then may we apply it to our non-Amish lives.

32

WHAT CAN THE AMISH TEACH US?

There are so many valuable lessons the Amish can teach us.

Separation. Many of my Louisiana friends and relatives didn't fully comprehend their dependence on "the grid" until Hurricane Katrina and its aftermath. Left without electricity or phone service for days, weeks, and in some cases months, they found themselves at the mercy of the weather (no air-conditioning!), the sunshine (no electric lights or television!), and the U.S. Postal Service (no e-mail!). And so much more.

Our lives depend on electricity from the first tones of the clock radio in the morning to the last light of the reading lamp at night. Sometimes when we look at the Amish, we're tempted to romanticize a life lived by candlelight dinners and woodstoves. However, having dined in an Amish home on a sweltering summer night when the lighting only added to the heat, I can say that the notion is highly overrated.

Rather than eliminating our dependence on the grid, our goal should be to moderate it. Taking a cue from the Amish, we can turn off the television, the computer, and the telephone far more often than we do. Once in a while, we should turn off the lights and fire up the candles. But may we never underestimate the value of turning those lights back on when we need them—not to mention basking in the warmth of our heaters or the coolness of our air conditioners as well.

Rules. Non-Amish parents might not communicate their household rules and expectations as formally as the Amish do in their *Ordnung*, but good parenting involves the creation and enforcement of various boundaries for our children. Just as the Amish periodically review their religious regulations and tweak or change them as necessary, we would do well to occasionally take a closer look at our own family rules and do the same.

Whether we loosen the reins a bit as our children mature or tighten up when they do not act responsibly, our rule making should be a dynamic process that addresses new challenges and changes in the light of our own family goals and principles. Once established, rules need consequences to remain effective, something the Amish have long understood and practiced.

Clothing and grooming. Most Christian denominations don't dictate their members' clothing choices, but make no mistake: Our clothes do reflect our belief systems, regardless. I'm always so dismayed when I see Christian boys sporting T-shirts with offensive messages or Christian girls wearing skimpy outfits, teeny bikinis, belly shirts, and super-low-cut jeans. I'm not a prude, but as the mother of two grown Christian daughters I can honestly say it is possible for teens to dress every bit as fashionably as their peers without having to cross the line into provocative or offensive outfits. It's not easy but it is possible—and most of all, it's important.

Stylish clothing that also happens to be modest says a lot about the wearer without saying a word, much as the simple *kapp*, dress, and apron of an Amish girl speaks for her.

Technology. Recently, our family was invited to stay at a small cottage in upstate New York. Perched on a hill overlooking Lake Champlain, the place was surrounded by all sorts of opportunities for water sports, hiking, and sightseeing. When we arrived, I told my husband I was glad to see the cottage had a television, as I had brought my Wii Fit just in case.

"Wii Fit?" he said, laughing. "How about we go outside and enjoy some *real* fit?"

It's easy to forget how simulated our lives are these days. Studying the Amish way of life reminds us that we can survive without all of the gadgets and devices we think are so indispensable.

We also need to keep in mind technology's dark side: cell phones that stop us from ever getting away from the office, texting that lets our teenagers carry on conversations with their friends while pretending to listen to their teachers, cable television that brings things into homes we would never invite.

Just as I put away the Wii Fit and picked up a canoe paddle at the lake, may we all pause now and then to evaluate our technological choices, weigh the pros and cons of each, and eliminate or moderate as necessary. By emulating the peaceful, technology-free evenings in Amish homes, may we bring peace and quiet back to our own.

The generations. Most Amish adapt appliances for their homes, so their kitchens may have refrigerators (powered by propane), their bathrooms may have plumbing (powered by compressed air), and their living rooms can be warm and cozy on the coldest winter nights (with heaters powered by bottled gas). Why, then, do they not heat their bedrooms? Surely they don't enjoy leaving the warmth of the hearth to go upstairs and slip between ice-cold sheets at bedtime, do they?

--- IN THEIR OWN WORDS ---

If you live an honest and upright life,
there is no need to "talk the talk."
Your life speaks for itself.

I asked that question of an expert on Amish life and was very surprised and impressed with his answer: "If the whole house is warm, what's to keep the children downstairs with their parents in the evenings? Everyone might want to go their own way, which can lead to the disintegration of the family."

In non-Amish homes, I don't recommend turning off the central heat for the sake of quality time, but a lot can be said for keeping all the fun stuff, such as video games and computers, out of the kids' rooms and in the common areas instead. It's safer for the kids, and it helps preserve the family unit by ensuring more together time on a regular basis.

In this way and many others, we can learn from the Amish and apply such lessons to our twenty-first-century lives.

Part Five:
SUPPLEMENTAL MATERIAL

It always amazed me that though Liesl and I were about the same age, she had married at nineteen, had begun having children soon after, and hadn't stopped yet. Currently, she and Jonah had five kids ranging in age from one to nine. I couldn't imagine a more horrifying prospect, but parenthood suited her very well.

"And you and Jonah? The two of you are happy?"

She looked at me strangely before answering that yes, they were fine, and why did I ask?

"I guess because I have enough trouble making a relationship work with just two of us. I can't fathom trying to do it with half a basketball team."

Liesl laughed melodically, saying it wasn't always easy with little ones underfoot, but they managed to do okay.

She and Jonah had always had seemed to be happily married, and I wanted to ask her what their secret was. But we lived in such different worlds that I had a feeling that, even if she could articulate it, whatever it was could never translate to my relationship with Heath—or with anyone else, for that matter.

"Someday I hope to have a marriage like that. Like yours. Like my parents," I said instead.

"Jah, I wish that for you too. But it will take the right person, especially because you are so much like me."

I smiled, knowing exactly what she meant. Our worlds couldn't be more different, but our personalities were very much the same.

—Excerpted from *Secrets of Harmony Grove*
by Mindy Starns Clark

BIBLICAL REFERENCES
FOR AMISH BELIEFS & PRACTICES

Adult baptism	Acts 2:38
Baptism	Matthew 3:5-6; 28:19-20; Mark 16:16; John 3:22-23; Acts 8:36-39
Church discipline	Matthew 7:13-14; John 15:1-10; 2 Corinthians 13:10; 1 Timothy 5:20; Titus 3:1-10
Church structure	1 Corinthians 4:17; Titus 1:6-9
Communion	Matthew 26:17-30; 1 Corinthians 10:16-17; 11:23-29
Community	Acts 2:44
Excommunication and shunning	Matthew 18:7-9; John 15:1-8; 1 Corinthians 5:11-13; 2 Thessalonians 3:14; Titus 3:10
Foot washing	John 13:1-17; 1 Timothy 5:10
Forgiveness	Matthew 6:14-15; Luke 6:37
Jesus Christ as the only foundation	1 Corinthians 3:11
Head coverings	1 Corinthians 11:3-16
Marriage roles	1 Corinthians 11:3,8-12; 1 Timothy 3:5
Mutual aid	Acts 2:45; 4:32
Peace and serenity	Matthew 6:25-34
Photographs	Exodus 20:4
Reinstatement after excommunication	Matthew 18:12-14; 2 Corinthians 2:5-11

Sabbath	Genesis 2:3; Exodus 20:8
Scripture	Proverbs 30:5-6; Romans 2:12; 2 Timothy 3:15-17
Selection of church leaders	Acts 1:24-26
Separation and nonconformity	Exodus 19:5; John 17:16; Acts 5:29; Romans 12:2; Titus 2:14; 1 Peter 2:9
Shunning	Romans 16:17; 1 Corinthians 5:11-13
Submission	Matthew 26:39-42; Titus 2:4-10

BIBLIOGRAPHY

Much of the information in *Plain Answers About the Amish Life* was gleaned from personal interviews, private tours, and the following sources.

Books

Bender, Harold S. *The Mennonite Encyclopedia*, 5 vols. Scottdale, PA: Herald Press, 1955-90.

Berend, Nina, and Elisabeth Knipf-Komlsi, eds. *Sprachinselwelten: The World of Language Islands*. Frankfurt, Germany: Peter Lang Publishing, 2006.

Burridge, Kate, and Werner Enninger, eds. *Diachronic Studies on the Languages of the Anabaptists*. Bochum, Germany: N. Brockmeyer, 1992.

Dewalt, Mark W. *Amish Education in the United States and Canada*. Lanham, MD: Rowman and Littlefield Education, 2006.

Fisher, Sara E., and Rachel K. Stahl. *The Amish School*. Intercourse, PA: Good Books, 1997.

Good, Merle, and Phyllis Good. *20 Most Asked Questions about the Amish and Mennonites*, rev. ed. Intercourse, PA: Good Books, 1995.

Hanley, Lucy. *The Amish in Words and Pictures*. Gettysburg, PA: Americana Souvenirs and Gifts, 1999.

Hostetler, John A. *Amish Life*. Scottdale, PA: Herald Press, 1983.

———. *Amish Society*, 4th ed. Baltimore, MD: Johns Hopkins University Press, 1993.

Hostetler, John A., and Gertrude Enders Huntington. *Amish Children: Education in the Family, School, and Community*, 2nd ed. New York, NY: Harcourt Brace and Jovanovich, 1992.

Johnson-Weiner, Karen. *Train Up a Child: Old Order Amish and Mennonite Schools*. Baltimore, MD: Johns Hopkins University Press, 2007.

Keffer, Gail. *Amish Paper Dolls*. New Wilmington, PA: Americana, 1996.

Kraybill, Donald B., ed. *The Amish and the State*, 2nd ed. Baltimore, MD: Johns Hopkins University Press, 2003.

———. *The Amish of Lancaster County*. Mechanicsburg, PA: Stackpole Books, 2008.

———. *The Puzzles of Amish Life*, rev. ed. Intercourse, PA: Good Books, 1998.

————. *The Riddle of Amish Culture*, 2nd ed. Baltimore, MD: Johns Hopkins University Press, 2001.

Kraybill, Donald B., and Carl Desportes Bowman. *On the Backroads to Heaven: Old Order Hutterites, Mennonites, Amish, and Brethren*. Baltimore, MD: Johns Hopkins University Press, 2002.

Kraybill, Donald B., and Steven M. Nolt. *Amish Enterprise: From Plows to Profits*, 2nd ed. Baltimore, MD: Johns Hopkins University Press, 2004.

Kraybill, Donald B., Steven M. Nolt, and David L. Weaver-Zercher. *Amish Grace: How Forgiveness Transcended Tragedy*. San Francisco, CA: Jossey-Bass, 2007.

McKusick, Victor. *Medical Genetic Studies of the Amish: Selected Papers, Assembled with Commentary*. Baltimore, MD: Johns Hopkins University Press, 1978.

Nolt, Steven M. *A History of the Amish*, rev. ed. Intercourse, PA: Good Books, 2003.

Nolt, Steven M., and Thomas J. Meyers. *Plain Diversity: Amish Cultures and Identities*. Baltimore, MD: Johns Hopkins University Press, 2007.

Plotnicov, Leonard. *American Culture: Essays on the Familiar and Unfamiliar*. Pittsburgh, PA: University of Pittsburgh Press, 1990.

Redcay, T.J. *The Old Order Amish in Plain Words and Pictures*. Gettysburg, PA: Americana Souvenirs & Gifts, 2000.

Scott, Stephen M. *Amish Houses and Barns*, rev. ed. Intercourse, PA: Good Books, 2001.

————. *The Amish Wedding and Other Special Occasions of the Old Order Communities*. Intercourse, PA: Good Books, 1988.

————. *Plain Buggies: Amish, Mennonite and Brethren Horse-Drawn Transportation*, rev. ed. Intercourse, PA: Good Books, 1998.

————. *Why Do They Dress That Way?* rev. ed. Intercourse, PA: Good Books, 1997.

Scott, Stephen M., and Kenneth Pellman. *Living Without Electricity*, rev. ed. Intercourse, PA: Good Books, 1999.

Shachtman, Tom. *Rumspringa: To Be or Not to Be Amish*. New York, NY: North Point Press, 2006.

Snyder, C. Arnold. *Anabaptist History and Theology: An Introduction*. Kitchener, ON: Pandora Press, 1995.

Stevick, Richard. *Growing Up Amish*. Baltimore, MD: Johns Hopkins University Press, 2007.

Stine, Eugene S. *Pennsylvania German Dictionary*. Birdsboro, PA: The Pennsylvania German Society, 1996.

Weaver-Zercher, David. *The Amish in the American Imagination*. Baltimore, MD: Johns Hopkins University Press, 2001.

Weaver-Zercher, David, and Diane Zimmerman Umble, eds. *The Amish and the Media*. Baltimore, MD: Johns Hopkins University Press, 2008.

Wesner, Erik. *Success Made Simple: An Inside Look at Why Amish Businesses Thrive*. San Franciso, CA: Jossey-Bass, 2010.

Wittmer, Joe. *The Gentle People: An Inside View of Amish Life*. Washington, IN: Black Buggy, 2007.

Yoder, Harvey. *The Happening: Nickel Mines School Tragedy*. Berlin, OH: TGS International, 2008.

Articles

"American Languages: Our Nation's Many Voices Online" http://csumc.wisc .edu/AmericanLanguages/search.php?sect=amish&state=pa.

Armstrong, Chris. "Christian History Corner: The Amish Come Knocking." *Christianity Today*, July 2004.

Ediger, Marlow. "Examining the Merits of Old Order Amish Education." *Education*, Vol. 117, 1997.

Gorsky, Eric. "Christian fiction: Buggies to Vampires." *Portland Press Herald*, July 18, 2009.

Greksa, Lawrence P., and Jill E. Korbin. "Key Decisions in the Lives of the Old Order Amish: Joining the Church and Migrating to Another Settlement." *Mennonite Quarterly Review*, 76, no. 4, July 2002.

Igou, Brad. "Back to School: Amish Style." *Amish Country News*. http://www .amishnews.com/amisharticles/backtoschool.htm.

Issenberg, Sasha. "The Simplest Life: Why Americans Romanticize the Amish." *Washington Monthly*, Vol. 36, October 2004.

Jacoby, Jeff. "Undeserved Forgiveness." *Boston Globe*, October 8, 2006.

Manni, Megan, and the Associated Press. "Gunman Reportedly Bent on 'Revenge' Kills Girls, Self at Amish School." Fox News, October 3, 2006.

McElroy, Damien. "Amish killer's widow thanks families of victims for forgiveness." The *Telegraph,* October 16, 2006.

Meyers, Thomas J. "The Old Order Amish: To Remain in the Faith or to Leave." *Mennonite Quarterly Review*, 68, no. 3. July 1994.

The Pennsylvania German Society. "A Very Brief Introduction to the Pennsylvania German Language."

Rifkin, Glenn. "The Amish Flock from Farms to Small Businesses." *New York Times*, January 7, 2009.

Sachs, Andrea. "Amish Romance Novels: No Bonnet Rippers." *Time*, April 27, 2009.

Young Center for Anabaptist an Pietist Studies. "Amish Migration Trends 2006-2010." http://www2.etown.edu/amishstudies/Migration_Trends.asp.

Films

Amish Values and Virtues: Plain and Simple, EIV Productions, 1994. 60 minutes, VHS.

An Amish Barn Raising, EIV Productions, 1994. VHS.

An Amish Country Adventure: Exploring the Back Roads of Holmes County, EIV Productions, 1994. 80 minutes, VHS.

Erwin, Jerry. *Who Are the Amish?* The People's Place, 30 minutes, theatrical viewing.

Ohio, Bennett-Watt Media, 2004. 60 minutes, DVD.

A Train Ride Through Amish Country, EIV Productions, 1995. VHS.

Walker, Lucy. *Devil's Playground*, Wellspring, 2002. 77 minutes, DVD.

Websites

American Languages. www.csumc.wisc.edu/AmericanLanguages/search_clip_type.php?clip_type=PennDutch.

Amish.Net. www.amish.net.

Wesner, Erik. www.AmishAmerica.com.

Young Center for Anabaptist and Pietist Studies at Elizabethtown College. www2.etown.edu/amishstudies/Index.asp.

Accommodations and Interview Facilitation

The Apple Bin Inn, Willow Street, Pennsylvania.

RESOURCES

For accurate and interesting information about the Amish and other Anabaptist groups, be sure to check out historical societies and information centers such as the ones listed below.

Amish and Mennonite
Heritage Center
Mailing address:
PO Box 324
Berlin OH 44610-0324

Street address:
5798 County Road 77
Millersberg, PA 44654
(330) 893-3192

Illinois Amish Interpretive Center
125 North County Rd 425 E
Arcola IL 61910
(217) 268-3599 or
1-888-45AMISH

Illinois Mennonite Historical and
Genealogical Society
Illinois Mennonite Heritage Center
675 State Route 116
Metamora IL 61548-7732
(309) 367-2551

Lancaster Mennonite
Historical Society
2215 Millstream Road
Lancaster PA 17602
(717) 393-9745

Mennonite Historical Library
Goshen College
1700 South Main Street
Goshen IN 46526
(574) 535-7000 or 1-800-348-7422

Mennonite Information Center
2209 Millstream Road
Lancaster PA 17602-1494
(717) 299-0954 or
Fax (717) 290-1585

Young Center for Anabaptist and
Pietist Studies
Elizabethtown College
One Alpha Drive
Elizabethtown PA 17022
(717) 361-1470

INDEX

20 Most Asked Questions about the Amish and Mennonites, 64, 153

Abroth, 122

academia, 134

accent, speaking with a, 85

acceptance, 56, 59

accomplishments, 129

accountability, 25, 28, 48

adult baptism, 46, 54, 118, 151

adultery, 47

affiliation, 8, 15-16, 21-23, 35-36, 42, 45, 55, 59

agriculture, 111

air-conditioning, 145

airplanes/air travel, 95

alcohol, 67, 114

alms, 42

Alsace, 54

America/American, 15, 33, 48, 55-56, 64, 83, 91, 97, 99, 105, 107, 115, 129

American Culture: Essays on the Familiar and Unfamiliar, 154

American Languages website, 156

"American Languages: Our Nation's Many Voices Online," 155

Amish and Mennonite Heritage Center in Berlin, OH, 157

Amish and the Media, The, 131, 155

Amish and the State, The, 153

Amish Barn Raising, An, 156

Amish board of education, 111

Amish Bride, The, 103

Amish Cheesy Potatoes recipe, 70

Amish Children: Education in the Family, School, and Community, 153

Amish Country Adventure: Exploring the Back Roads of Holmes County, An, 156

Amish culture, 130-131, 138

Amish Education in the United States and Canada, 153

Amish Enterprise: From Plows to Profits, 154

Amish Family Cookbook, The, 71

"Amish Flock from Farms to Small Businesses, The," 155

Amish genes, value of, 75

Amish Grace: How Forgiveness Transcended Tragedy, 48, 138, 154

Amish Houses and Barns, 154

Amish in the American Imagination, The, 155

Amish in the City, 133

Amish in Words and Pictures, The, 153

"Amish killer's widow thanks families of victims for forgiveness," 155

Amish Life, 153

Amish life, 63-68, 141

Amish Mafia, 133

Amish mentality, 129

Amish Midwife, The, 127

"Amish Migration Trends 2006-2010," 156

Amish Nanny, The, 13

Amish of Lancaster County, The, 153

Amish organization, 35, 36

Amish Paper Dolls, 153

Amish Paradox: Diversity and Change in the World's Largest Amish Community, An, 23

"Amish Romance Novels: No Bonnet Rippers," 156

Amish School, The, 153

Amish Society, 153

Amish taxi, 95

Amish tours, 134

Amish Values and Virtues: Plain and Simple, 156

Amish Wedding and Other Special Occasions of the Old Order Communities, The, 154
Amish-owned businesses, 63, 90
Amish-related myths, 8, 131, 133
Amish-related organizations, 11
Amish, definition of, 15-17
Amish, lessons to be learned from, 145-147
Amish, reasons for being, 141-143
Amish.Net, 156
AmishAmerica.com, 27, 156
AmishReader.com, 12
Anabaptism/Anabaptist, 16, 53-54, 118, 134
Anabaptist History and Theology: An Introduction, 154
Anabaptist movement, 53
Andy Weaver Amish, 55
animal, 99, 105
announce, 121
answering machine, 92
antiques, 101
apostles, 39
Apple Bin Inn, 156
appliances, 66, 147
apron, 80, 82
archery, 100
arithmetic, 111
Armstrong, Chris, 155
art, 111
articles, 155
artwork, 54, 64-66, 78, 80-82, 89-90, 93-95, 109, 126
Ashkenazi Jews, 75
Associated Press, 135
assurance of salvation, 21
auctions, 101
Ausbund, 43, 84
authority, 20, 26, 37, 112
autism, 73
availability of farm land, 97
ax, 107
babies, 99
"Back to School: Amish Style," *Amish Country News,* 155

ban, 47, 50
banks, 67
baptism, adult, 46, 54, 118, 151
baptism/baptize, 11, 16, 27, 37-38, 42, 46-47, 49-50, 53-54, 57, 91, 103, 113-114, 117-119, 122, 151
barefoot, 78, 107
barn raising, 27, 101
barn, 27, 36, 42, 54, 87, 90, 92, 101, 122, 127, 141
bathroom, 66, 109, 147
batteries, 89, 94
Beachy Amish, 55, 59
beard, 80-81
becoming Amish, 113
bed-and-breakfast, 130
bed courtship, 115
bedroom, 114-115
beer bashes, 114
behavior, 106, 112
beliefs/belief system, 12, 16, 19-26, 29, 33, 35-36, 53-54, 74, 117-118, 146
belt buckle, 79
bench wagon, 94
benches, 41-42, 94, 122
Bender, Harold S., 153
Berend, Nina, 153
Berks County, 55
Beverages, 69
Bible, 22, 29, 31, 33, 38-39, 42-43, 54, 85, 122
Bible, Luther, 85
Bible, translation, 43
Biblical references for Amish beliefs and practices, 11, 151-152
bibliography, 153-156
bicycles, 46, 95
bills, 26, 88, 92
birth control, 73
birth rate, 57
birthday parties, 100
birthing center, 73
bishop, 22, 26, 36-39, 41-42, 47, 117, 119, 121-123, 135

black prayer covering, reason for, 80

blending in, 55

blinkers, 94

board games, 99-100

bonnet, 80

bonnet, illustration, 81

bookkeeping, 112

born again, 21

Boston Globe, 138

bottled gas, 89, 147

boundaries, 36, 145

Bowman, Carl Desportes, 154

brain damage, 140

bras, 81

bread, 69

breadwinner, 107

Breaking Amish, 133

bride, 121-124

broadfall trousers, 78, 79, 82

Brunstetter, Wanda, 101

Budget, 28

buggy color, 94

buggy shops, 63

buggy types, photographs of, 94

buggy, 34, 93-94, 101

bundling, 115

burial clothing, 125

burial, 126

Burridge, Kate, 153

bus, 109

business failure rate, 98

business principles, 106

business, 84, 90, 98, 106, 130

buttons, 78-80

cake, 100, 123

calculator, 89

call log, 92

calories, 69

cameras/photography/photographs, 7, 33, 92, 94, 107, 151

camping, 99

Canada, 15-16, 35-36, 57

candies, 101

candles, 101

canning, 69, 101

cape, 80

car, 59, 87-88, 93-95, 114, 118

card games, 99-100

casket, 125-126

Catholic/Catholicism, 19, 53

celebrations, 100-101, 122-123

celery, 124

cell phone, 90-91, 114, 146

cemetery, 126

central authority, 22

certification, 110

chainsaw, 89

Charming Nancy, 54

checking account, 67

chickens, 69

child labor, 33

child safety, 134

children/childhood, 11, 16, 26, 28, 34, 41-42, 57, 61, 63-65, 73, 78, 82, 84, 91, 95, 101, 105-113, 117, 129, 134, 137-139, 142, 145-147, 149

chores, 26, 63-65, 79, 82, 99, 105-106

chow chow, 70

Christian Aid Ministries, 24

Christian character, 109

Christian faith, 7, 43, 54, 113-114, 119, 135

"Christian Fiction: Buggies to Vampires," 155

"Christian History Corner: The Amish Come Knocking," 155

Christlike/Christlikeness, 21, 45, 77, 98, 141

Christmas cards, 101

Christmas program, 101

Christmas trees, 101

Christmas, 101, 110

church and state, 53-54

church authority, 47

church buildings, 36, 42, 59

church leaders/leadership, 11, 16, 22, 36-39, 46, 53, 55, 88, 90, 94, 114, 119, 121, 123, 129, 138, 152

church members, 19, 26-27, 35-36, 38-39,

46-47, 49-50, 53, 78, 95, 113, 115, 117-119

church service, 27, 36-38, 41-43, 46, 66, 84, 94, 119, 122-123, 126

church structure, 151

cigar/cigarette smoking, 67

classes, 117-119

classmates, 25

classroom, 111

clean/cleaning, 64, 97, 105, 124

Clinic for Special Children, 74-75

clothesline, 65

clothing colors, 79, 82

clothing storage, 82

clothing stores, 81

clothing, 11, 15-17, 45, 59, 64, 77-82, 118, 125, 127, 131, 141, 146

clothing, commonalties between districts, 78

clothing, for babies, 82

clothing, for children, 82

clothing, for church, 79

clothing, for married, 78

clothing, for unmarried, 78

clothing, for work, 79

clothing, illustration, 82

coal, 89

cockscomb flowers, 65

coffee, 67, 69

colonies/colonists, 55, 83

comfort food, 69

commerce, 84

commitment, 7, 46, 50, 114

communion, 37-39, 42, 46, 53, 119, 151

community, 7, 20, 23, 25-29, 31-32, 45, 50, 58-59, 67, 74, 84, 87-88, 90-91, 93, 101, 105-106, 109-110, 112-113, 118, 121-122, 124-126, 129, 138, 140-142, 151

companion/companionship, 64, 108

compassion, 55

compliance, 118

compressed air, 89, 147

compromise, 95, 110

compulsory military service, 54

computer, 66, 88, 90, 111, 129, 142, 145, 147

concordance, 38

confession, 47-49

conglomerate, 67

congregation, 22, 31, 35, 37-39, 41, 42, 46, 53, 66, 121-122

conscientious objectors, 34

conservative/conservatism, 66, 70, 73-74, 79, 80-81, 114-115

construction work, 98

conversion, 23, 50, 91, 129

convert to the Amish faith, 129

cook/cooking, 98-99, 105-106

copy machines, 89

corn, 97

correspondence course, 111

cosmetics, 125

cotton, 79

council/council meeting, 42, 46

counseling, 75

court, 32-33

courting buggy/courting wagon, 94, 114

courting/courtship, 94, 114-115, 121, 124

cow, 69, 107

craftsmanship, 63, 66

creativity, 112, 130

credit card, 67

crime rate, 48

crime, 48, 54, 138-139

critical analysis, 112

criticism, 138

crops, 63, 67, 97

croquet, 99

cult, 19

culturally isolated groups, 75

culture clash, 133

culture, 20, 131, 138

curiosity, 55-56, 135

curriculum, 111

curtains, 65

dairy farms, 97

dairy products, 69

dancing, 100

danger, 48, 107

dates/dating 114, 121

deacon, 37-38, 119, 121

death, 11, 26, 28-29, 54, 125-126

decision making, 25, 31, 38-39, 46, 90-91, 113, 118

decorations, 66-67, 101

demographics, 11

Demut, 106

denomination, 19-22, 146

Deutsch, 83

Devil's Playground, 133, 156

devotions, 101, 106

Dewalt, Mark W., 153

diabetes, 75

Diachronic Studies on the Languages of the Anabaptists, 153

dialect, 83-84, 130

diapers, 82

Die Ernsthafte Christenpficht, 85

diesel, 66, 89

digital technology, 90-91

dignity, 45, 108, 142

diploma, 112

disagreements, 55, 140

discipline, 16, 37, 47, 49-50, 53, 115, 142, 151

disputes, 27, 48, 55

districts, 16, 22-24, 28, 35-38, 42, 45-47, 49, 58-59, 66-67, 70, 73-74, 77-81, 87-89, 91-92, 94-95, 99, 111, 114-115, 118, 122, 123, 140

diversity, 55

divine appointment/divine lot, 16, 38-39, 119

division, 15, 29, 36, 46, 51, 55

divorce, 124

DNA, 75

doctor/physician, 73-74

doctrinal purity, 53

documentaries, 133

Dordrecht Confession of Faith, 118

dress, 20, 30, 77, 79-82

drive/driving/driver, 87-88, 95

driver's license, 114

drugs, 114

dryer, 64, 87

Dutch Blitz, 100

duties, 37-39, 122

dwarfism, 75

e-mail, 7, 88, 145

Easter Island, 75

Ediger, Marlow, 155

education limits, 110, 112

education, 15, 32-33, 45, 59, 74, 98, 110-112, 129, 131, 141

eggs, 69

Eicher, Jerry 71

Eicher, Tina, 71

Eighteen Articles, 15

eighteenth century, 15, 115

eighth grade, 110-112

elder, church, 47

elderly, 107-108, 142

electric/electricity/electronics, 20, 30, 59, 65-66, 87-89, 114, 129, 141, 145

Elkhart/LaGrange, 35

embalm, 125

emergencies, 92

engagements/engagement announcement, 121

English, 8, 38, 83-85, 111, 118, 130, 132

English, learning to speak, 84

Englisher, 130

Enninger, Werner, 153

entertainment, 99-101, 142

entrepreneurs/entrepreneurship, 63-64, 98

Erwin, Jerry, 156

eulogy, 126

Europe, 59

evangelizing, 23

"Examining the Merits of Old Order Amish Education," 155

excommunication, 19, 37-38, 47, 49, 53, 119, 151

expansion, 11, 15, 57-59, 65-66, 107

exploitation, 56, 132-133

fabric, 77, 79-80, 138
Facebook, 12
facial hair, 78, 80
factory, 63, 97
faith culture, 17, 20
faith/Christian faith, 7-9, 11, 13, 15-17,
    19-20, 23, 29, 37, 43, 46-47, 53-54, 64,
    84, 113-114, 119, 122, 129, 135
family planning, 73
family wagon, 94
family, 20, 35, 41-42, 46-47, 50, 57, 61,
    63-66, 73-74, 81, 87-88, 92-94, 98, 101,
    105-108, 110, 114, 118, 121-122, 124-126,
    138-139, 141-142, 145-147
fancy, 8, 79, 87, 93, 126
fans, 89
farm equipment, 89-90, 107
farm, illustration, 65
farm/farmer/farming, 17, 26-27, 39,
    58-59, 63, 65, 89, 90, 92, 95, 97, 105-
    107, 111, 125, 127, 129-131
farmers' market, 97
farmhouse/farmland, 58, 63, 65, 97
fascination with the Amish, 131-132
fat content, 69
feed grinder, 90
fellowship, 28, 36, 123, 141
fiction authors, 134-135
fiction, 7, 17, 134-135, 142
films/film industry, 132, 156
financial aid, 26, 30, 31, 38, 142
first grade, 110-111
Fisher, Sara E., 153
fishing, 99
flashlight, 89
flirting, 100, 114
flowers, 65, 126
food, 61, 66, 69-71, 100-101, 122, 124,
    131-132
foot washing, 42, 53, 151
For Richer or Poorer, 133
Ford, Harrison, 132
forgive/forgiveness, 47-49, 134, 137-140,
    151

formal education, 15, 110
founder effect, 75
France, 54
freedom of religion, 33
freedom, 15, 33, 53, 83, 111, 113-114, 130
friends/friendship, 25, 28, 32, 47, 63, 84,
    92, 99-101, 114, 121-122, 124-126, 141-
    142, 146
frolic, 101
fry pie, 70
fun, 99, 105
funeral, 26-27, 37, 125-126, 138
furniture making, 63, 98
furniture, 17, 63, 66, 131-132
games 100, 123
Garden of Gethsemane, 20
garden, 64, 66, 69, 124
gasoline, 87, 89-90, 93
Geauga County, 121
GED, 112
generations, 65, 105, 147
generator, 87
genetic disorders, 75
genetics, 75
Gentle People: An Inside View of Amish Life,
    The, 155
geography/geographical area, 35, 111
German Reformed Church, 83
German, 16, 38, 41, 43, 83-84, 106, 111,
    130
Germany, 83
gifts, 100-101, 123
goal(s), 88, 112
God's will, 20-22, 32, 39, 142
Good, Merle and Phyllis, 64-65, 153
Gorsky, Eric, 155
Goshen College, 98, 157
gossip, 28, 91
Gould, Leslie 13, 103, 127
government, 30, 33-34, 53-54
grace, 19, 21, 108, 138-139, 142
grade levels, 109
grain, 97
grammar, 111

graven image, 92
graves, 126
graveyard, illustration, 126
Greksa, Lawrence P., 155
grid, 88-89, 145
grief, 139
grill, 89
groceries, 64
groom, 121-124
grooming, 77, 80, 146
Grossdaadi Haus, 107, 142
group singings, 100, 114, 123
Growing Up Amish: The Teenage Years, 115, 154
Gulf Coast, 24
"Gunman Reportedly Bent on 'Revenge' Kills Girls, Self at Amish School," 155
guns, 68, 137
hair-cutting attacks, 48
hair/hairstyles, 78, 80, 118
Hanley, Lucy, 153
"Happening, The," 139
Happening: Nickel Mines School Tragedy, The, 155
harvest, 69
hat brim, 78-79, 122
hat press, 82
hat, 78-79, 82, 122
hay bailer, 90
head covering/kapp, 78, 80-81, 103, 122, 146, 151
headstone, 126
health care, 33
health insurance, 74
health, 73-75
heat/heater, 66, 90, 147
heaven, 21-22
heritage, 16, 54
High German, 41, 43, 83-84
high tech, 112
historical societies, 134, 157
History of the Amish, A, 154
history, 11, 13, 16, 20, 29, 48, 53-56, 77, 88, 93, 111, 131, 137-138

holidays/holiday activities, 100-101, 110
holistic, 73
Holmes County, 7, 35
holy kiss, 119
home birth, 74
home-based business, 98, 106
home, 13, 15, 27, 30, 35, 42-43, 46, 54, 57, 63-66, 70, 73-74, 78, 81-83, 87, 89-91, 93, 98, 100-101, 106-107, 110, 112-115, 122, 124-126, 129-130, 133, 139-140, 142, 145-147
home, signs of an Amish, 65
homemaker, 107
Homestyle Amish Kitchen Cookbook, 71
honeymoon, 124
hooks and eyes, 79
horse and buggy, 15-16, 65, 67, 93, 95, 105
horse and buggy, illustration, 93
horse, 90, 93, 107-108
hospital, 26, 73-74, 125
Hostetler, John A., 134, 153
hot water heaters, 89
house, 15, 36, 42, 65, 87, 92, 107-108, 127, 147, 154
housecleaning, 97
how to use this book, 11-12
humility, 20, 25, 77, 79, 87, 93, 106, 126
hunting, 68, 69, 99
Huntington, Gertrude Enders, 153
Hurricane Katrina, 24, 145
Hurst, Charles, 23-24
hydraulics, 90
hymnal/songbook, 39, 43, 84
hymns/songs, 41, 43, 84, 100-101, 122-123, 126
ice cream, 100, 123
Iceland, 75
Igou, Brad, 155
Illinois Amish Interpretive Center in Arcola, IL, 157
Illinois Mennonite Historical and Genealogical Society in Metmora, IL, 157
immigrants/immigration, 54-55, 115
in-law suite, 108

independence/independent thinking, 112-113

Indiana, 35, 55, 58, 83

individuality, 77, 112, 130

industrialization, 55

infant baptism, 53-54

inline skates, 89

innovation, 87

instrument, 41, 43, 100

insurance, 26, 30-31, 88, 93

interaction, 11, 32, 36, 91

intermarriage, 36

Internet, 59, 88, 90-91

Iowa, 55

Issenberg, Sasha, 155

issues/problems, 46-48, 56, 106, 131, 135

Jacoby, Jeff, 155

jail, 110

Jesus Christ as the only foundation, 21, 151

Jesus, 19-22, 32, 151

jewelry, 77, 81

jobs/job market, 58-59, 106

Johnson-Weiner, Karen, 153

judging others, 137

jury duty, 33

kapp/head covering, 78, 80-81, 103, 122, 146, 151

Keffer, Gail, 153

kerosene, 66, 89, 94

"Key Decisions in the Lives of the Old Order Amish: Joining the Church and Migrating to Another Settlement," 155

King James Version, 43

Kingpin, 133

kiss the bride, 123

kitchen, 66, 106

Knipf-Komlsi, Elisabeth, 153

Korbin, Jill E., 155

Kraybill, Donald B., 31, 48, 134, 138, 153-154

Lake Champlain, 146

lamps, 89

Lancaster County, 7, 8, 35, 37, 55, 58, 67, 75, 91, 95, 97, 101, 110, 121, 132

Lancaster Mennonite Historical Society in Lancaster, PA, 157

land prices/rising cost of, 56, 58-59, 97

language, 11, 16, 41, 83-85, 111, 129-131

lapels, 78-80

laundry, 64

lawnmower/lawn equipment, 16, 89, 101

lawsuits, 32

leader/leadership, 11, 16, 22, 36-39, 46, 53, 55, 88, 90, 94, 114, 119, 121, 123, 129, 138, 152

learn/learning, 43, 51, 63, 95, 97, 105-106, 112, 117-118, 129, 139, 147

leaving an Amish settlement, 58, 113

leaving the Amish faith, 50, 58, 113, 119

leisure, 99-101

letters, writing, 28, 99

Lewis, Beverly, 135

liberal, 114

lifestyle, 11, 15, 20, 21, 25, 30, 34, 36, 55, 61, 69, 75, 97, 105-106, 110, 132, 135, 141

lights, 66, 89, 94, 101, 145

limits on education, 110, 112

link to buggy photographs, 94

link to hear Pennsylvania Dutch, 84

link to photographs, 107

literacy, 84

litigation, 32

livestock, 27

living hope, 21

Living Without Electricity, 154

loan, 67

lot/divine lot, 38-39, 119

Louisiana, 145

low tech, 88

lumber, 101

Luther Bible, 43, 85

Lutheran, 83

luxury, 129

lyrics, 43

mail order, 66

makeup, 81

manual labor, 63

manufacturing, 90

Manz, Felix, 54

maple syrup urine disease, 75

market wagon, 94

market wagon, illustration, 94

marriage outside of faith, 122

marriage, 11, 27, 38, 50, 81, 115, 121-124, 149, 151

Martin Luther Bible, 43, 85

martyr, 29, 54, 84

Martyrs Mirror, 13, 54

mate, 100, 113

McConnell, David, 23-24

McElroy, Damien, 155

McGillis, Kelly, 132

McKusick, Victor, 154

meal, 63-64, 101

media, 11, 85, 132-135

medical care, 73-75

medical expenses, 74, 142

Medical Genetic Studies of the Amish: Selected Papers, Assembled with Commentary, 154

medical research, 75

medicine, natural, 73

meet an Amish person, how to, 130

Meidung, 47

Mennonite Central Committee, 24

Mennonite Encyclopedia, The, 153

Mennonite Historical Library at Goshen College in Goshen, IN, 157

Mennonite Information Center in Lancaster, PA, 157

Mennonite, 15-17, 24, 53-54, 59, 75, 83

mental health care, 75

mental illness, 75, 134, 138

Mexico, 74

Meyers, Thomas J., 154-155

midwife/nurse-midwife, 74, 127

military, 33, 54, 78, 80

milk, 67, 115

minister's wagon, 94

minister/ministry, 26, 28, 36-39, 41-42, 117, 119, 121-122, 126

missions/missionaries, 23, 59

modesty, 20, 77-78, 81, 146

monetary dependence, 30

money, 67, 77

mortician, 125

mother and child, illustration, 80

mother, 91, 98, 106-107, 139, 146

mothers, working outside of home, 98, 107

Mount Eaton Care Center, 74

Mount Gretna, 75

Mountain Dew, 67

mud sale, 101

municipal authority, 94

municipal issues, 58

museum, 99

music, 43, 88, 100, 111

mustache, 80

mutual aid, 25, 151

myth of the pastoral, the, 131, 133

naphtha, 89

National Amish Steering Committee, 33

National PTA, 112

natural disaster, 26

natural gas, 90

neighbors, 36, 109, 142

New American Almanac, The, 28

New Hope, 140

New International Version, 43

new normal, 139

New York Times, 98

New York, 55, 58

news/news industry, 28, 100, 132-133

Nickel Mines, 48, 134, 137-140

Nolt, Steven M., 48, 134, 138, 154

nomination of leaders, 38-39

nonresistance, 31, 33-34, 68

noodles, 69

North America, 15-16, 55

nurse-midwife, 74

nursing homes, 107

obedience, 21, 32, 43, 77, 88, 93, 112, 129

obsession with the Amish, 131-132

occupations, 59, 97-98, 141

Ohio, 7, 24, 28, 35, 48, 55, 57, 74, 121, 156

Old Order Amish in Plain Words and Pictures, The, 154

"Old Order Amish: To Remain in the Faith or to Leave, The," 155

oldest Christian songbook, 84

On the Backroads to Heaven: Old Order Hutterites, Mennonites, Amish, and Brethren, 154

Ontario, 55

opposite sex, 114-115

oral tradition, 46

orange triangle, 94

ordination, 28, 37

Ordnung, 45-46, 50, 66, 78, 114, 118, 140, 145

ostracism, 56

outdoor activities, 100

outhouse, 65, 109

outside world, 11, 46, 84, 88, 110, 113-114, 127, 129-130

overcrowding, 56, 63

PA Dutch Country, 101

pacifism/passive resistance/pacifist, 16, 32, 55

Palatine dialect, 83

pants, 78, 82

parents/parenting, 42, 65, 91, 94, 105-106, 108-109, 112-115, 117, 119, 122, 124, 142, 145, 147, 149

parochial school, 109

partying, 113-114, 118

patriarchal democracy, 38

peace/peacefulness/serenity, 20, 46, 88, 91, 141-142, 151

peculiar people, 20

Pellman, Kenneth, 154

penmanship, 111

Pennsylvania Dutch, 41, 69, 83-84, 113, 129

Pennsylvania Dutch, link to example of, 84

Pennsylvania German Dictionary, 154

Pennsylvania, 7, 35, 48, 55, 58, 74-75, 97, 132, 137

People of Preservation, A, 133

persecution, 29, 54, 56, 97

personal relationship with Jesus Christ, 21-22

Philhaven, 75

phone shanty, 92

phonebook, 92

photo identification, 33

photographs/photography, 33, 92, 94, 107, 151, 155

physical education, 111

pickup wagon, 94

pickup/market wagon, illustration, 94

pie, 69

pigs, 69

pinafore, 82

pins, 80

pipe smoking, 67

Plain Buggies: Amish, Mennonite and Brethren Horse-Drawn Transportation, 154

Plain Diversity: Amish Cultures and Identities, 154

play/playtime, 65, 82, 99, 105, 141

Plotnicov, Leonard, 154

plumbing, 65-66, 89, 147

Pocket Guide to Amish Life, A, 11

police/police officer, 33, 48, 137

political office, 32

politics, 38

Pomerene Hospital, 74

pony/pony cart, 95

pope, 22

population, 57, 97

potty training, 82

pranks, 123

pray/prayer, 20, 38, 41, 47, 61, 64, 80-81, 85, 106, 111, 122-123, 126

prayer book, 41, 85

prayer covering, 80-81

preaching, 37, 41

pregnancy, 115

premarital sex, 115

pride, 21-22, 36, 45, 77, 87, 93-94, 129

privacy, 94, 115

problems/issues, 46-48, 56, 106, 131, 135
produce stand, 106
prohibited subjects, 111
pronunciation, 85
propane, 66, 87, 89-90, 147
Protestant Reformation, 53
protestant, 19, 151
psychiatrist/psychologist/psychology, 75, 139
PTA, 112
public displays of affection, 123
public school, 30, 109
public transportation, 95
public utilities, 15
publish an engagement, 121
publishing industry, 132
Puzzles of Amish Life, The, 153
quality time, 147
quilting bee, 101
quilts/quilting/quilt making, 98, 101, 107, 131
quote from Amish, 20, 23, 38, 67, 81, 92, 147
Raber's Almanac, 28
rape/sexual assault, 48
rare blood type, 75
rare disorders, 75
reading, 28, 38, 41-42, 63, 99, 111, 123, 126, 134-135, 142-145
reality television, 133
reception, wedding, 123
recidivism, 48
recipe, 70
reconciliation, 47
Redcay, T.J., 154
reflective tape, 94
refrigerator, 66, 89, 147
regulations, 8, 21, 30, 37, 45-46, 53, 55, 77-78, 145
reinstatement, 37-38, 151
relationships with non-Amish, 32
relatives, 28, 36, 59, 88, 99, 124, 126
religious freedom, 83, 111
repentance, 47, 49-50

reprimand from church elder, 47, 49
researchers of Amish, 16, 35
resources for further study, 11-12, 134, 157, 161
respect, 25, 112
responsibilities, 64-65, 105, 112, 114
restaurants, 70, 97
retention rate, 57
revenge, 139, 159
Riddle of Amish Culture, The, 31, 154
Rifkin, Glenn, 98, 155
rubber tire, 90
rules, establishing, 88
rules/restrictions, 15, 19-20, 36, 38, 45-48, 50, 78-80, 87-89, 91, 93-95, 99, 113, 118, 140-141, 145-146
Rumspringa, 49, 113-115, 117, 118
Rumspringa: To Be or Not to Be Amish, 154
rural, 15, 54, 110
Sabbath, 42, 152
Sachs, Andrea, 156
safe/safety, 33-34, 48, 73, 94-95, 106-108, 134, 142, 147
safety markings on buggies, 94
safety net, 142
salvation, 19, 21
satisfaction, 64, 141
savings account, 67
schitz pie/schnitz pie/shitz pie, 70
scholar, 101, 109
school board, 111
school budget, 111
school bus, 109
school shooting, 137-140
school subjects, 111
school term lengths, 110
school, 30, 34, 43, 48, 65, 78, 82, 84, 98, 100-101, 106, 109-112, 134, 137, 141
school, illustration, 109
schoolhouse, 101, 109, 137
science, 111
scooter, 95
scooter, illustration, 95
Scott, Stephen M., 154

scrapple, 70

Scripture, 19-22, 25, 29, 32-33, 38-39, 47, 51, 80-81, 92, 97, 126, 137, 142, 151-152

secrecy, 121

Secrets of Harmony Grove, 149

selection of church leaders, 16, 38-39,152

self-defense, 33, 68

self-discipline, 112, 115

sentence construction, 85

separation, 20-21, 29-32, 43, 93, 124, 145, 152

Sermon on the Mount, 20

sermon, 38, 41, 54, 83, 122-123, 126

settlement, 16, 28, 32, 34-35, 55, 58-59, 63, 121, 123, 131, 135

settlement, choosing a new location for, 58

sew/sewing/sewing machine, 64, 81, 87, 89, 106

sex, 51, 114-115

sexual assault/rape, 48

Shachtman, Tom, 154

Shadows of Lancaster County, 61

shirts, 79, 82

shoes, 78-79

shoofly pie, 70

shopping, 64, 66, 69, 132

shunning, 19, 47, 49-51, 53, 114, 118-119, 151, 152

Shunning, The, 135

Simons, Menno, 53

"Simplest Life: Why Americans Romanticize the Amish, The," 155

simplicity, 20-21, 43, 66, 77, 88, 97, 142

sin, 47, 51, 121, 137

singing, 41, 100, 114, 123, 141

sink, bathroom, 66

skates/skating, 89, 100

sledding, 99-100

sliding walls, 66

smoke alarms, 89

smoking, 67, 114

sneakers, 78

Snyder, C. Arnold, 154

Social Security, 30, 33-34

social studies, 111

socializing, 100-101

soda, 67, 69

softball, 99-100

songbook/hymnal, 39, 43, 84

songs/hymns, 41, 43, 100-101, 122-123, 126

special needs, 109

spelling, 111

spiritual leaders/leadership, 11, 16, 22, 36-39, 46, 53, 55, 88, 90, 94, 114, 119, 121, 123, 129, 138, 152

split, 53, 55

sports/sport teams/sporting events, 99-100, 146

Sprachinselwelten: The World of Language Islands, 153

spring wagon, 94

Stahl, Rachel K., 153

statistics, 16, 35, 57

Stevick, Richard, 115, 134, 154

Stine, Eugene S., 154

stockings, 78

stove, 66, 89, 145

straight pins, 80

straw hat, illustration, 67

Streng Meidung, 50

subjects prohibited in school, 111

submission, 20-21, 43, 46-47, 50, 77, 81, 88, 93, 112, 129, 152

Success Made Simple: An Inside Look at Why Amish Businesses Thrive, 63, 155

suit, 79, 82

Sunday school, 42, 117

Supreme Court, 32, 110

surprise parties, 100

surrender, 20-21, 43

suspenders, 78-79, 82

swimming, 100

Swiss Anabaptists, 54

Swiss church, 53

Swiss dialect, 84

Swiss government, 53

Switzerland, 53

symbol, 27, 77, 81, 93

synthetic fabric, 79

taxes, 30

taxi, 95

teacher/teaching, 42, 109-111, 142

teaching, by parents, 65, 105-106, 112, 117, 142, 145

technological adaptations/devices, 17, 66, 89-90, 147

technology, 11, 16, 30, 45, 46, 59, 66, 87-92, 98, 118, 129, 146-147

teens/teenagers/youth, 28, 42, 84, 91-92, 100, 106, 112, 113, 114, 115 117, 118, 123

telephone, 30, 66, 87, 91-92, 129, 142, 145

television, 66, 88, 132, 145-146

temptation, 45, 88, 93

tenon joint construction, 27

texting, 91, 146

thee and thou, 85

theology, 11, 20, 39, 42, 59, 106, 141

therapist, 75

thrift, 20, 66, 77, 88, 93, 98

tires, 90

tobacco, 67, 97

toilet, 66

tolerance, 56

tools, 27, 63, 89

"Top 10 Things Teachers Wish Parents Would Do," 112

torture, 29, 54

tour guide services, 134

tourism bureau/tourist information center, 101, 130

tourism, 11, 56, 58, 101, 130, 131-135

tourist traps, 132

tractors, 90-91

trades, 97

tradition, 20, 25, 29, 46, 69, 73, 87, 97, 107, 125

traditional roles, 63-65, 107, 151

traffic, 94

tragedy, 48, 137-140, 154

Train up a Child: Old Order Amish and Mennonite Schools, 153

translation, Bible, 43

transportation, 11, 15, 30, 45, 93-95

travel, 23, 74, 93, 95, 99, 124, 131

triangles, on buggies, 34, 94

typewriter, 89

typical Amish childhood, 105

typical day for an Amish child, 65

typical day for an Amish man, 63

typical day for an Amish woman, 64

Umble, Diane Zimmerman, 131-133, 155

undergarments, 81

"Undeserved Forgiveness," 155

Uneheliche beischlaf, 115

unions, 32

United States, 15-16, 28, 33, 35-36, 57, 74

unity, 22, 30, 46

U.S. Supreme Court, 32, 110

vacation, 99

vaccination, 73

value system/values, 7-8, 17, 20, 22, 25, 77, 87-88, 97-98, 109, 111-112, 135

vanity, 77

Varozza, Georgia, 71

"Very Brief Introduction to the Pennsylvania German Language, A," 155

vests, 79

victim, 139-140

video games, 147

violence, 48, 133-134, 137

visitation, funeral, 125

vocabulary, 83

voice mail, 92

volleyball, 99-100

volunteer, 24, 122-123, 125, 134

vote, 31, 39, 47

vow, 46-47, 114, 119, 123

wages, 63

wagon, 42, 94, 114

wake, funeral, 125

walk-a-mile, 123

Walker, Lucy, 156

war, 29, 55

washing machine, 64, 89-90, 123

washing machine, illustration, 64

water heater, 89

water, 66, 69, 103, 119, 146

wealth, 98

weapons, 68

Weaver-Zercher, David L., 48, 131-134, 138, 154, 155

websites, 28, 156

wedding attendants, 122

wedding gifts, 124

wedding reception, 123

wedding ring, 81, 123

wedding, 37, 121-124, 154

wedding, decorations, 124

Weir, Peter, 132

Wesner, Erik, 27, 63-64, 67, 155

white prayer cover, reason for, 80

Who Are the Amish? A Train Ride Through Amish Country, 156

whoopie pie, 70

Why Do They Dress That Way?, 154

why they are Amish, 141

Wii Fit, 146-147

wild behavior, 113

wild game, 69

Willems, Dirk, 13

wind, 66, 89

windmill, illustration, 90

window treatments, 65

Wisconsin v. Yoder, 32, 110

Wisconsin, 58

wisdom, 25, 45, 108

Witness, 132-133

witnessing, 23

Wittmer, Joe, 155

women, 28, 38, 61, 64, 73-74, 78-82, 97, 101, 115

wood-peg mortise, 27

wood, 63, 66, 89-90, 107

woodstove, 145

wool, 79

word of mouth, 100, 126

work ethic, 97-98, 105, 141

work frolic, 101

work, 23-24, 27, 33, 37, 42, 63, 64, 79, 95, 97-99, 101, 105-107, 112, 122, 125, 129, 141

workers' compensation, 30

workplace, 63, 91

works, salvation through, 21

worship, 15, 25, 35, 38, 41-43, 59, 84, 122, 141

www.amishfaq.com, 84, 94, 107

Yoder, Harvey, 155

Young Center for Anabaptist and Pietist Studies, 16, 35, 156-157

Youngie, 123

youth/teens/teenagers, 28, 42, 84, 91-92, 100, 106, 112-115, 117-118, 123

Zeugnis, 121

zoning issues, 31, 33, 58

zoo, 99

Zurich, 54

NOTES

Chapter 2—Beliefs

1. Erik Wesner, "Ask an Amishman: What do the Amish think about Jews?" March 16, 2009, http://amishamerica.com/ask-an-amishman-what-do-the-amish-think-about-jews/.

2. Charles Hurst and David McConnell, *An Amish Paradox: Diversity and Change in the World's Largest Amish Community* (Baltimore, MD: The Johns Hopkins University Press, 2010), 67.

3. Ibid., 64.

Chapter 3—Community

1. Erik Wesner, "What happens at an Amish barn raising?" September 25, 2011, http://amishamerica.com/what-happens-at-an-Amish-barn-raising.

2. Robert Rhodes, "For the Amish, almanacs help keep the year in order," *Mennonite Weekly Review,* January 12, 2004, http://www.mennoworld.org/2004/1/12/amish-almanacs-help-keep-year-order/?print=1.

Chapter 4—Separation

1. Donald B. Kraybill, *The Riddle of Amish Culture* (Baltimore, MD: Johns Hopkins University Press, 2001), 275.

Chapter 9—Rules

1. Andrew Welsh-Huggins and John Seewer, "Hair Attacks for Ohio Amish to Seek Outside Help," October 15, 2011, http://www.msnbc.msn.com/id/44915054/#.UOoGg6X5J-B.

2. Donald B. Kraybill, Steven M. Nolt, and David L. Weaver-Zercher, *Amish Grace: How Forgiveness Transcended Tragedy* (San Francisco, CA: Jossey-Bass, 2007), 34.

3. Welsh-Huggins and Seewer, "Hair Attacks for Ohio Amish to Seek Outside Help," October 15, 2011, http://www.msnbc.msn.com/id/44915054/#.UOoGg6X5J-B.

Chapter 12—Expansion

1. Young Center for Anabaptist and Pietist Studies, Elizabethtown College, "Amish Population Trends 2012, One-Year Highlights," http://www2.etown.edu/amishstudies/Population_Trends_2012.asp.

2. Ibid.

Chapter 13—Amish Life

1. Erik Wesner and Donald B. Kraybill, *Success Made Simple: An Inside Look at Why Amish Businesses Thrive* (San Francisco, CA: Jossey-Bass, 2010), 2.

2. Ibid., 156.

3. Merle Good and Phyllis Good, *20 Most Asked Questions About the Amish and Mennonites* (Intercourse, PA: Good Books, 1995), 54.

4. Ibid., 54.

5. Ibid., 57.

6. Erik Wesner, "Do the Amish Drink," May 25, 2007, http://amishamerica.com/do_the _amish_dr/.

Chapter 20—Occupations

1. Glenn Rifkin, "The Amish Flock from Farms to Small Businesses," January 7, 2009, http://www.nytimes.com/2009/01/08/business/smallbusiness/08sbiz.html?pagewanted= all&_r=0.

2. "Part Two: An Amish America Q-and-A with a Lancaster County Amishman," December 2, 2008, http://amishamerica.com/an-amish-america-qanda-with-a-lancaster-county amish man-part-two/.

Chapter 21— Free Time, Vacations, and Entertainment

1. Pennsylvania Dutch Convention & Visitors Bureau, "Mud Sales in Lancaster County," http://www.padutchcountry.com/towns-and-heritage/amish-country/amish-mud-sales .asp.

Chapter 23—School

1. Family Education Staff, "Top 10 Things Teachers Wish Parents Would Do," http://school .familyeducation.com/parents-and-teacher/38781.html?detoured=1.

Chapter 29— Tourism and the Media

1. Diane Zimmerman Umble and David L. Weaver-Zercher, *The Amish and the Media* (Baltimore, MD: The Johns Hopkins University Press, 2008), 6.

2. Ibid., 21.

3. Erik Gorski, "Christian Fiction: Buggies to Vampires," July 18, 2009, http://www.press herald.com/archive/christian-fiction-buggies-to-vampires_2009-07-17.html.

Chapter 30—Tragedy and Forgiveness

1. Jeff Jacoby, "Undeserved Forgiveness," October 8, 2006, http://www.jeffjacoby.com/5858/ undeserved-forgiveness.

2. Donald B. Kraybill, Steven M. Nolt, and David L. Weaver-Zercher, *Amish Grace: How Forgiveness Transcended Tragedy* (San Francisco, CA: John Wiley & Sons, Inc., 2007), 176.

3. Ibid., 180.

ABOUT THE AUTHOR

Plain Answers About Amish Life is Mindy's twentieth book with Harvest House Publishers. She is the coauthor, with Leslie Gould, of the bestselling Women of Lancaster County series, which includes the Christy-award-winning *The Amish Midwife* as well as *The Amish Nanny, The Amish Bride,* and *The Amish Seamstress.* Mindy's other Amish-themed works include the mystery novels *Shadows of Lancaster County* and *Secrets of Harmony Grove,* and the gift book *Simple Joys of the Amish Life.*

Mindy is a popular speaker and playwright as well as a former singer and stand-up comedian. She lives near Valley Forge, Pennsylvania, with her husband and two daughters.

Visit Mindy's websites at www.mindystarnsclark.com and www.amishfaqs.com.

ABOUT THE ARTIST

Amy Hanson Starns has worked as a graphic artist for more than 25 years, designing logos, album covers, magazine editorials, advertisements, and more. She has two grown children and lives in Flagstaff, Arizona. Amy earned her degree in Fine Arts from California State University.